Easy AIR FRYER Bakes

*This book is dedicated
to my family near
and far.*

Easy AIR FRYER Bakes

Lucy Parissi

Photography by Ant Duncan

MICHAEL JOSEPH

PENGUIN MICHAEL JOSEPH

UK | USA | Canada | Ireland | Australia
India | New Zealand | South Africa

Penguin Michael Joseph is part of the Penguin Random House group of companies
whose addresses can be found at global.penguinrandomhouse.com

First published 2024
001

Set in Goldplay
Design and Art Direction by Georgie Hewitt
Food Styling by Katie Marshall
Colour reproduction by AltaImage Ltd
Printed and bound in Italy by L.E.G.O. S.p.A

The authorized representative in the EEA is Penguin Random House Ireland,
Morrison Chambers, 32 Nassau Street, Dublin D02 YH68

A CIP catalogue record for this book is available from the British Library

ISBN: 978–0–241–69656–9

The recipes in this book involve the use of an air fryer. Please read the instruction manual to ensure that you operate the air fryer in accordance with the instructions and be careful when handling parts of the air fryer that can become hot to avoid burns. Every effort has been made to ensure that the information contained in this book is complete and accurate. It is the reader's responsibility to use their judgement when preparing recipes to ensure that they are aware of any dietary restrictions, allergies or health concerns. Neither the author nor the publisher shall be liable or responsible for any loss or damage allegedly rising from any information or suggestion in this book.

www.greenpenguin.co.uk

Breakfast
BAKES

Everyday
BAKES

Cookies
AND BARS

Holiday
BAKES

Celebration
CAKES

Delectable
DESSERTS

Savoury
BAKES

Bread &
YEASTED DOUGH

Introduction

I grew up in Athens, Greece, where cooking and sharing food is central to living. My mum would always cook and bake up a storm when hosting parties and gatherings at our house. Her creations were always made with love and tasted incredible. Helping my mum in the kitchen, especially when she was baking, delighted me as a child.

I moved from Athens to the UK to study graphic design when I was seventeen and very quickly my culinary horizons opened up to cuisines from around the world. To this day nothing makes me happier than preparing and sharing food with family and friends.

I started my blog *Supergolden Bakes* in 2012 to document and share my kitchen misadventures. It was just a hobby at first, but cooking, baking and photographing my creations brought me immense joy. So much so that it gradually transitioned from a side hustle to my full-time occupation.

Baking, in particular, is still something I turn to whether I am feeling happy, sad, anxious or filled with indecision (almost always then). Reading through a recipe, gathering, measuring and mixing ingredients has an intense calming effect. I can feel my heartbeat slow down. My anxious thoughts take a back seat for a blissful hour or so and I finally feel more in control. It can't be a coincidence that during the pandemic our collective response was to find solace in the sweet comfort of baking.

EASY AIR FRYER BAKES

Do you own an air fryer? Chances are the answer is yes. Do you use it to cook chips, fish fingers, jacket potatoes and very little else? I'd guess you're also nodding, albeit reluctantly.

I was once the same. As a food blogger I was lucky enough to test a few air fryers way back in 2013. At the time they were loud, incredibly bulky and built sort of like a UFO.

I admit that we only used ours to cook frozen chips and very little else. It was only recently that I discovered that modern air fryers are not just an economical alternative to the traditional oven; they are, in fact, hugely versatile. So I started experimenting with recipes and soon realized that air fryer meals are tastier, quicker and healthier. My readers responded enthusiastically to the recipes as soon as I posted them and clamoured for more.

Since baking is a passion of mine, I began to tentatively test some of my recipes in the air fryer. The first time I baked an air fryer cake I was absolutely thrilled with the results. Pretty soon I was air frying bread, cinnamon rolls, muffins, pies, pavlovas and so much more.

Easy Air Fryer Bakes brings together a selection of eighty sweet and savoury recipes inspired by bakes from around the world. From cookies and pies to celebration cakes, cheesecake, bread, spanakopita and baklava, there's a treat for every occasion.

What is an air fryer?

An air fryer is essentially a small but powerful oven, which cooks food by circulating hot air. They are compact, easy to use and clean, cheap to run and surprisingly versatile. Anything an oven can cook, air fryers can usually cook quicker and, dare I say it, better!

GET TO KNOW YOUR AIR FRYER

The recipes in this book have been tested using basket-type air fryers, which tend to be the most popular. Although air fryer brands and models vary in size and shape, their basic functions are usually similar. Read through your manual to familiarize yourself with the basics, which I will quickly summarize here for you:

- Position your air fryer on a heat-resistant surface with sufficient space around and behind it to allow for hot air to vent through the back.

- Remember that the air fryer basket will be very hot after baking, so make sure to place it on a heat-resistant surface or a suitable liner.

- Avoid using low-calorie cooking sprays as they can damage the interior. Buy a couple of glass spray bottles to use with your choice of oil.

- You can use baking paper, air fryer liners and kitchen foil in your air fryer, as long as you remember to always weigh it down or clip it first. If the paper is not weighed down, it can be pulled into the fan and can easily burn or damage your air fryer.

BAKING IN AN AIR FRYER

As soon as you ignore the 'fryer' part and think of your air fryer as a mini-oven you will embrace its versatility. You can bake almost anything in an air fryer and the only limit is your imagination.

It is so much quicker. Lengthy preheating will be a thing of the past – your air fryer is ready to use in a fraction of the time. Saving energy and cutting down on bills are huge perks, but there's a bit of a learning curve when you first start using your air fryer. Since air fryers are so much smaller than traditional ovens, they tend to run hotter. There's also some inconsistency between brands that you need to take into account. Certain models are so powerful that you might need to adjust the recommended cooking temperature, dropping it down by a few degrees. Others cook slower and run less hot, in which case you can turn the temperature up a notch.

It's also worth remembering that since the heat comes from the top, a cake can look perfectly done halfway through the cooking time. Do not be fooled – always use a toothpick to test for doneness or, better yet, a digital thermometer. You can easily pull out the basket to check on your bake without compromising it – just be gentle when opening and closing. Once you have got the hang of baking in your air fryer, making these tweaks will become second nature.

LIST OF USEFUL TOOLS AND EQUIPMENT

- selection of silicone cake tins of various sizes (20/15/13cm), muffin tin, silicone muffin cases
- digital scales and measuring spoons
- digital thermometer
- silicone liners, reuseable baking liners & paper liners

- hot dish lifting tool
- metal pudding moulds
- small metal baking tins
- cookie cutters, pastry cutters, piping tips, silicone cupcake cases
- mini chopper/food processor
- small clips
- cake release spray
- cake leveller
- square metal cake tin
- silicone cake tin
- air fryer wire rack
- loaf tin & cake barrel tin

How to use this book

There's a wide range of recipes inside, from cakes and muffins to breads and desserts. Start by making one of the easier recipes, such as Banana Bread on page 54 or the Vanilla Cupcakes on page 49. This way you can familiarize yourself with air fryer baking and get to know your model.

Check through the ingredients list to make sure you have all that you need. Do you own the right type and size of baking tin and does it fit comfortably in your air fryer basket?

Read through the method and make sure you have enough time to prepare and cook your chosen bake, allowing for proving or chilling where appropriate.

Gather your ingredients and equipment and get your bake on – and afterwards make a note about whether you needed to adjust the temperature or cooking time. It is very likely that you will need to take that into consideration for other recipes as well.

If you are baking for a special occasion, I would always recommend testing the recipe before the big day. Birthday cakes can always be baked up to a day or two in advance and kept wrapped at room temperature until you are ready to frost them.

I have tried to keep all the recipes in this book as straightforward as possible, simplifying and stripping down the steps. While most of the recipes are easy, there are a few ambitious bakes to try once you become more confident, such as Macarons (page 83) or Brioche (page 202).

ESSENTIAL EQUIPMENT

Since air fryer baskets vary in size and shape you will probably need to invest in a few tools, especially if you are a keen baker. You can buy bundles of air fryer products that include a variety of accessories.

Bear in mind that silicone cake tins, muffin tins, baking liners and so on can also be used to make all kinds of recipes – not just cakes and bakes. Anything that can be used in an air fryer can also be used in an oven.

A NOTE ON INGREDIENTS

Baking is much less forgiving than cooking when it comes to substituting ingredients. Stick to the recipe ingredients and make sure that items such as flour, baking powder, bicarbonate of soda and yeast are fresh.

All the recipes use medium eggs. Eggs and butter should ideally be at room temperature, unless specified, to prevent the batter curdling. Margarine, on the other hand, can be used straight from the fridge!

I like using good-quality baking chocolate chips in my baking. You can also use a 60% cocoa chocolate bar, cut into small pieces, instead of the chips.

Use unwaxed lemons and oranges for zesting, giving them a good scrub first.

If you like using flowers to decorate your cakes, make sure they are edible flowers that are free of pesticides.

Baking tips & troubleshooting

THE BAKING TEMPERATURE

Air fryers usually have a variety of settings programmed in. Most of the recipes in this book use the baking setting, usually 160°C, adjusting the temperature as needed. See table below.

As with ovens, some air fryers run hotter than others. The recipes have been tested in several air fryers and I have provided the baking temperature that works best across the board.

I have said this before but it's worth repeating: you might need to adjust the temperature by up to 10 degrees depending on your air fryer. Bear in mind that your air fryer will already be hot if you are baking in batches, so you might need to shorten the cooking time on the second and third batch.

Avoid overcrowding – always allow for space so that air can circulate freely. If you crowd the food in the basket, it will take longer to cook and may not crisp up.

RECIPE TYPE	TEMPERATURE	NOTES
BREAD	Bake setting 180–200°C	Requires flipping over to brown the bottom. Internal temp. 98–99°C
ENRICHED BREAD & ROLLS	Bake setting 160–180°C	Cover with foil if browning too quickly, making sure to secure the foil. Internal temp. 93–96°C
CAKES & CUPCAKES	Bake setting 150–170°C	Cover with foil if browning too quickly, making sure to secure the foil. Bake until a toothpick comes out clean. Internal temp. 96–98°C
COOKIES & BARS	Bake setting 150–180°C	Cookies will firm up as they cool. May need to reduce temperature/ cooking time after first batch. Internal temp. 93–96°C
SAVOURY BAKES	Air fryer setting 180–200°C	Avoid overcrowding for crisp results!
MERINGUE & MACARONS	Bake setting 120–90°C	Reduce temperature if meringue is browning

THE TOOTHPICK TEST

Use a toothpick or a skewer (or even a dry spaghetti noodle) to test whether your cake is done. Insert in the middle of your bake 4–5 minutes before the end of the cooking time. If it comes out covered with wet batter, you will need to cook for longer before testing again. Bake until your tester comes out clean or with a few crumbs. An instant-read digital thermometer can be used in the same way, with the additional perk that you can check your bake has reached the optimum baking temperature.

Allow cakes and cookies to cool for a few minutes in the air fryer basket before lifting out on to a wire rack to cool.

BREAD AND YEASTED BAKES

Baking bread – actually anything involving yeast – used to fill me with dread. It seemed such a long-winded and mysterious process filled with potential pitfalls. My first few attempts were disappointing, if not outright disastrous. But I persisted, and I am so glad I did. There's nothing to fear provided your yeast is fresh. I like to use rapid-rise, or instant, yeast, which is mixed in with the flour and doesn't require activation.

Remember that heat kills yeast, so always make sure that any liquid used in the recipe is at room temperature and never any hotter.

The rising and proving times specified in the recipes vary greatly depending on how warm it is in your kitchen. You can use the air fryer to prove the dough; some models even have a proving setting. To do this, cover your bowl with greased cling film and place in the air fryer basket with the appliance turned off. Just don't forget it is in there if you are preheating the air fryer for a different recipe!

Since air fryer heat comes from above, you will need to flip your loaf over so it can brown evenly. You can test whether it is done by tapping the underside to check it sounds hollow.

If your bake is browning too quickly on top, you can cover it with foil, placing a rack on top to make sure it doesn't fly off.

DON'T FORGET!

Always weigh down paper liners, foil and so on when cooking in an air fryer. I like to clip down any overhanging paper in loaf tins so that it doesn't blow into the bakes.

Certain air fryer fans are so powerful that lighter bakes, such as cupcakes and biscuits, can literally take off. Nothing is more disappointing than opening the basket and being greeted by sad mangled cupcakes! I recommend using sturdy baking cases or placing muffins in metal pudding moulds so that they keep their shape.

1

Breakfast **BAKES**

Blueberry Muffins

Forget overpriced coffee-shop blueberry muffins because these are SO MUCH better. Fluffy, fragrant, moist and packed with plump blueberries. Yum!

DRY INGREDIENTS
320g plain flour
150g caster sugar
30g soft light brown sugar
3 tsp baking powder

WET INGREDIENTS
265ml vanilla kefir or vanilla
   yogurt
65g unsalted butter or
   coconut oil, melted
3 eggs
2 tsp vanilla extract
200g fresh blueberries

FOR THE TOPPING
1 tbsp unsalted butter, cold
   and cubed
1 tbsp soft light brown sugar
1 tbsp demerara sugar
1 tbsp plain flour
1 tsp cinnamon

- Add all the dry ingredients to a large mixing bowl and stir to combine.

- Combine all the wet ingredients except the blueberries in a measuring jug and pour into the dry ingredients.

- Fold together gently until the batter is well mixed and no dry streaks remain.

- Combine all the topping ingredients in a bowl and rub together to create a crumble-like texture.

- Put a scoop of batter in each of the cases and push several blueberries into the batter. Top with a little more batter and a few more blueberries. (Do not overfill.)

- Spoon some of the crumble over the top of each muffin.

- Preheat the air fryer for 5 minutes at 180°C. Place the muffins in the air fryer basket (in batches if necessary). Bake for 20–25 minutes or until the muffins are well risen and a toothpick inserted in the middle comes out dry.

- Cool slightly before serving.

NOTE Store blueberry muffins in an airtight container at room temperature for up to three days. Line the container with paper towels and place the muffins on top in a single layer.

Churro French Toast Sticks

PREP 10 mins
AIR FRY 6 mins
SERVES 6-8

Forgive the cultural mish-mash because these French toast sticks are beyond delicious! They're as light as air, and crunchy and addictive in the best possible way.

FOR THE FRENCH TOAST

500g brioche loaf

180ml double cream

40ml semi-skimmed milk

2 tbsp maple syrup, plus extra to serve

1 tbsp caster sugar

1 tsp vanilla extract

1 tsp orange zest (optional)

FOR THE CINNAMON SUGAR

150g granulated sugar

50g demerara sugar

½ tbsp ground cinnamon

- Slice the brioche loaf into 2cm thick slices and cut each slice into three to create sticks. If you can, leave the bread out so it can dry out a little. This recipe works best with slightly stale bread.

- Combine the double cream, milk, maple syrup, sugar, vanilla and orange zest, if using, in a wide shallow bowl.

- Briefly dip a bread stick into the cream mixture, turning to coat it. Place on a wire rack set over a baking tray so any excess can drip off. Repeat with the rest of the bread sticks.

- Combine the ingredients for the cinnamon sugar in a separate bowl.

- Preheat the air fryer to 195°C for 3 minutes and place a liner in the air fryer basket. Dip the sticks in the sugar, turning them to coat fully, and place on the liner spaced slightly apart. You will need to cook these in batches, allowing space between them so that the air can circulate.

- Cook for 6 minutes, turning over halfway, or until the bread is golden and crisp.

- Transfer to a wire rack to cool – the bread will become firmer as it cools.

- Serve immediately for breakfast or brunch with a drizzle of maple syrup.

NOTES

* Serve drizzled with melted chocolate for dessert.

* Instead of a brioche loaf (see page 202 to bake your own), you can use the Orange & Cardamom Challah Bread on page 210 or the Hot Cross Bun Loaf on page 88.

Blueberry Baked Oats

Who doesn't like a healthy breakfast that tastes a little bit like cake?
These baked oats are packed with fruit, fibre, seeds and just a hint
of sweetness. Delicious served warm with a drizzle of maple syrup.

1 medium banana (peeled
   weight 90–95g)

3 tbsp brown sugar

1 tbsp maple syrup, plus
   extra to serve

1 tsp vanilla extract

1 egg

150g porridge oats

1 tsp baking powder

1 tsp cinnamon

pinch of salt

100g fresh blueberries

2 tbsp mixed seeds
   (pumpkin, sunflower,
   sesame, etc.)

1 tbsp demerara sugar

- Blitz the banana, sugar, maple syrup, vanilla and egg in a food processor or mini chopper until liquidized.

- Add the oats, baking powder, cinnamon and salt to a mixing bowl. Stir in the banana mixture and leave for about 10 minutes to allow the oats to absorb some of the liquid.

- Line a 20cm square tin with baking paper. Pour the batter into the tin and level.

- Top with the blueberries, pushing them slightly into the oats.

- Sprinkle with the seeds and sugar and bake in a 170°C preheated air fryer for 40–45 minutes, or until the oats are set and the top is golden.

- Lift out of the air fryer on to a wire rack and leave to cool completely before serving.

- Slice into squares and serve with a little maple syrup.

NOTE Keep in the fridge for up to three days, reheating in a microwave or the air fryer if preferred.

Three-Cheese Breakfast Casserole

PREP 15 mins
BAKE 50-55 mins
SERVES 8-10

Ultra-rich and packed with eggs, prosciutto and three types of cheese, this savoury bread-and-butter pudding can be customized to include your favourite ingredients. It's a great way to use up slightly stale bread, turning it into a make-ahead breakfast or brunch, perfect for a crowd.

450g white bread, cubed (e.g. Beginner's Overnight Sourdough, see page 216)
180g prosciutto
300ml semi-skimmed milk
8 eggs
2 tbsp unsalted butter, melted
2 tbsp mustard
2 tsp mixed Italian herbs
1 tsp garlic granules
½ tsp salt
½ tsp freshly ground black pepper
200g Comté cheese (or strong Cheddar)
100g Gruyère cheese
50g grated mozzarella

FOR THE TOPPING
2 tbsp unsalted butter, cold and cubed
1–2 tbsp grated mozzarella

- Line a 20cm square tin and mist with cake release or grease with butter.

- Slice the bread into small even cubes (of about 1cm). Remove any pieces of hard crust.

- Finely chop the prosciutto or blitz it in a mini chopper.

- Add the milk, eggs, melted butter, mustard, mixed herbs, garlic granules, salt and pepper to a large mixing bowl. Lightly beat together with a fork or balloon whisk.

- Grate the cheeses and add to the bowl, stirring to combine.

- Add the bread and stir a few times so it starts to absorb the eggs and milk mixture.

- Pack the bread down into the prepared tin, cover and chill for 2 hours or even overnight. Preheat the air fryer to 180°C for 3 minutes. Dot the casserole with the cubed butter and add a little grated cheese. Cover the tin with the foil tucked snugly around it so it doesn't fly off.

- Bake for 40 minutes. Remove the foil and bake for a further 10–15 minutes or until the casserole is golden and crunchy on top. A skewer inserted in the middle should come out clean and the internal temperature should be above 70°C when checked with an instant-read thermometer.

- Leave it to cool for 10 minutes before slicing and serving with a drizzle of Hollandaise sauce.

NOTE Slice and freeze the casserole for up to three months. Toast from frozen and serve.

Pancakes

PREP 10 mins
COOK 10-11 mins
MAKES 12-16

You can prepare the batter for these fluffy buttermilk pancakes the night before and then air fry a batch or two the following morning for breakfast or brunch. Jazz these up with chocolate chips or sprinkles on special occasions.

WET INGREDIENTS

460ml vanilla kefir or
 buttermilk
2 eggs
2 tbsp butter, melted
1 tbsp maple syrup
1 tsp vanilla extract

DRY INGREDIENTS

260g plain white flour
2 tbsp sugar
1 tsp baking powder
1 tsp bicarbonate of soda
¼ tsp salt

SERVING SUGGESTIONS

butter
maple syrup
fresh berries

- Place the kefir, eggs, melted butter, maple syrup and vanilla in a mixing bowl. Stir to combine.

- Sift in the flour, sugar, baking powder, bicarbonate of soda and salt. Gently fold the dry ingredients into the wet until the batter is smooth. Leave this to rest for 20 minutes.

- Mist 10cm silicone moulds with cake release. Make sure they are well greased. Add a scoop of batter in each and place in the air fryer basket.

- Cook for 5–6 minutes at 180°C – the tops should be bubbly and slightly golden. Use tongs to invert the pancakes directly into the basket so that they are flipped over. Cook for a further 5 minutes or until golden. Transfer to a wire rack.

- Repeat until you have used up all the batter, making sure to grease the moulds every time otherwise the pancakes will stick.

- Serve with maple syrup and fresh berries or your favourite toppings.

Pecan Danish Pastries

PREP 25 mins
PROVE & CHILL 5+ hrs
BAKE 12-15 mins
MAKES 8-9

Freshly baked Danish pastries are a joy forever . . . or for the few seconds before you demolish them. This is one of the more complex and time-consuming recipes in the book and all the more rewarding for it. Remember that the dough needs to chill for a few hours, so it's best to make it the night before you need it.

FOR THE DOUGH

250g plain flour, plus extra
  for dusting and rolling
65g white bread flour
70g caster sugar
1½ tsp rapid-rise yeast
½ tsp salt
230g unsalted butter, cold
  and cubed
180ml whole milk
1 egg
1 egg beaten with a little
  milk, for the egg wash
pearl sugar (optional), for
  topping

FOR THE FILLING

100g pecans
3 tbsp dark brown sugar
30g unsalted butter, cold
6 tbsp maple syrup
1 tsp vanilla extract
1 tsp cinnamon
pinch of salt

FOR THE MAPLE GLAZE

4–5 tbsp icing sugar
1 tbsp maple syrup
1 tsp vanilla extract
hot water, if needed

Make the dough

- Combine the two types of flour, sugar, yeast and salt in the bowl of your food processor.

- Add the cubed butter and pulse a few times until the mixture resembles chunky breadcrumbs. You want the butter to remain in pea-sized pieces.

- Mix the milk and the first egg together in a measuring jug.

- Tip the flour mixture into a large bowl and add the milk/egg mixture. Gently combine until the dough just comes together – don't overwork it.

- Line your worktop with two large pieces of cling film. Tip the dough on to it and use the cling film to squash the dough into a square. Put in the freezer for 30–45 mins or in the fridge for a few hours until it becomes firm but still pliable.

- Liberally dust your worktop and rolling pin with flour. Roll your dough out to a rectangle roughly three times as long as it is wide. Fold the short sides of the dough into the middle, using a pastry scraper to help you if it's sticky.

- Rotate the dough by a quarter turn. Fold the short ends towards the middle. Flip the dough over so the seams are underneath. Roll it out again, repeating steps 5–7 a few times until the dough starts to become elastic.

Recipe Continues Overleaf
• • •

- Wrap the dough twice with cling film and rest in the fridge for a minimum of 4 hours or overnight. You are now ready to use it.

Make the filling

- Put all the ingredients in the small bowl of a food processor or mini chopper. Pulse until you have a coarse paste. Set aside until needed.

Shape the pastries

- Cut the dough in half. Keep the piece you aren't using in the fridge until needed.

- Dust your worktop and rolling pin with flour. Roll the dough out to about 5mm thick and trim the edges.

- To create pinwheels, cut the dough into squares and make small cuts from the corner towards the centre of each square. Place one heaped teaspoon of the filling in the middle and fold every other point in towards the centre.

Bake the pastries

- Transfer to an air fryer liner, cover loosely with greased cling film and let them rise at room temperature for 30 minutes.

- When you are ready to bake, brush egg wash over the pastries and sprinkle with a little pearl sugar if using. You will need to bake in batches of three to four.

- Preheat the air fryer to 170°C. Place a wire rack in the basket and position the liner over it. Bake for 12–15 minutes, depending on size, until puffed and golden.

- Leave the pastries in the basket (out of the air fryer) to cool slightly before transferring to a wire rack.

- Mix all the ingredients for the glaze and drizzle over the pastries before serving.

NOTE Check after 7 minutes whether the pastries are browning too quickly – you can cover them loosely with foil if they are. Remember to weigh down the foil if using.

Custard Buns

PREP 20 mins
BAKE 30-35 mins
MAKES 8 large buns

This recipe is inspired by Bienenstich (bee sting cake) and is one of my all-time favourite bakes. It's soft and pillowy, filled with vanilla custard and topped with a crunchy honey and almond topping . . . simply irresistible!

FOR THE FILLING

50g custard powder
400ml whole milk
100g granulated sugar
2 tsp vanilla bean paste
50g unsalted butter, cubed

FOR THE STARTER

120ml whole milk
20g (2 level tbsp) bread flour

FOR THE DOUGH

120ml whole milk
1 egg
55g unsalted butter, softened
1 tsp vanilla bean paste
350g white bread flour
70g caster sugar
2 tsp rapid-rise yeast
½ tsp salt

FOR THE EGG WASH

1 egg, lightly beaten with 1 tsp water

FOR THE TOPPING

75g unsalted butter
75g granulated sugar
1 tbsp honey
1 tbsp double cream
100g flaked almonds

Make the custard filling

- Place the custard powder, milk, sugar and vanilla in a saucepan. Simmer over a low heat, stirring constantly until the custard thickens.

- Remove from the heat and stir in the butter until it melts and the custard is smooth. If it is a bit lumpy, you can pass it through a sieve. Cool before using, ideally for a few hours or overnight in the fridge.

Make the starter

- Place the milk and flour in a saucepan and stir over a medium heat with a small balloon whisk until the whisk leaves a trail on the surface and you have a thick paste. Cover with cling film unless using straight away to prevent a skin forming on the surface.

Make the dough

- Add the milk to the saucepan containing the starter and heat until small bubbles appear around the edge. Allow this to cool until it is tepid and stir in the egg, butter and vanilla. The butter should melt in the residual heat.

- Measure the flour, sugar, yeast and salt into the bowl of a stand mixer fitted with a dough hook. Stir to combine.

- Pour in the contents of the saucepan while mixing on a low speed. You should have a shaggy, sticky dough.

- Increase the speed slightly and mix for 2–4 minutes, or until the dough becomes elastic and starts to form a ball around the dough hook.

- Stretch a small piece of dough between your fingers – if it forms a see-through membrane without tearing it is ready to use.

Recipe Continues Overleaf
• • •

First rise

- Mist the bowl with oil or brush with butter. Cover with greased cling film and leave to rise for 60–90 minutes or until doubled (depending on room temperature).

Second rise

- Deflate the dough and tip on to a lightly floured worktop. Leave to rest for a few minutes, then roll out to form a 40x28cm rectangle. Trim the edges if needed.

- Use a palette knife to spread the custard in an even layer over the dough. (You may have leftover custard.)

- Roll up the dough, starting with the long edge, to form a log, brushing the dough with melted butter as you go. Pinch the edge to seal.

- Transfer the log on to a baking liner or baking paper and chill in the freezer for 30 minutes or so. This will help you cut the buns without the custard oozing out. Use unflavoured dental floss to cut the dough into eight 5cm-thick buns.

- Place the buns on two greased air fryer liners, 4 per liner, spaced slightly apart. Brush with the egg wash.

- Cover loosely with greased cling film and leave to rise for 45–60 minutes or until the buns are puffy and risen.

Make the topping

- Prepare the topping while the buns are rising. Combine all the ingredients apart from the almonds in a saucepan.

- Let it bubble away for 5 minutes, stirring frequently, until it turns a little darker. Take it off the heat and mix in the flaked almonds. Cool slightly before using.

Bake

- Place a tablespoon of the almond topping on top of each bun. You don't need to spread it out as it will melt while baking.

- Bake at 155°C for 30–35 minutes, covering with foil after 12 minutes (weigh down the foil with a wire rack). Cool in the air-fryer basket for 5 minutes before lifting out.

Cinnamon Apple Muffins

PREP 10 mins
BAKE 20–25 mins
MAKES 6

These Cinnamon Apple Muffins are, in a word, awesome! They're deliciously scented, incredibly moreish and super easy to make. Serve them slightly warm and allow their intoxicating fragrance to wrap you in a hug.

80ml coconut oil, melted and cooled
2 eggs
200g apple sauce
150g light brown sugar
200g plain flour
1½ tsp baking powder
3 tsp cinnamon
¼ tsp salt
pinch of freshly ground nutmeg

- Combine the oil, eggs, apple sauce and sugar in a mixing bowl.
- Sift in the flour, baking powder, cinnamon, salt and nutmeg. Use a spoon to fold the dry and wet ingredients together until no dry streaks of flour remain.
- Divide between six tulip muffin cases (place them inside pudding moulds) and air fry for 20–25 minutes at 170°C or until they pass the toothpick test.
- Eat these as soon as they are cool enough to handle – they are impossible to resist!

NOTE Store in a paper towel-lined airtight container for up to three days. Reheat in the mircrowave or the air fryer to serve.

Cinnamon Rolls

PREP 30 mins
PROVE 2 hrs 15 mins
BAKE 23–25 mins
MAKES 10

My daughter tasted these cinnamon rolls and exclaimed, 'What black magic are you using to make these? They are incredible!' There's no magic but there is a secret to these super-soft and addictive rolls – a starter made with water and flour. Trust me when I say these really are the BEST-EVER cinnamon rolls!

FOR THE STARTER

120ml whole milk

20g bread flour (2 level tbsp)

FOR THE DOUGH

120ml whole milk

1 egg

55g unsalted butter,
  softened

1 tsp vanilla bean paste

350g white bread flour

50g caster sugar

2 tsp rapid-rise yeast

½ tsp salt

FOR THE FILLING

100g granulated sugar

2 tbsp cinnamon

75g unsalted butter, melted

FOR THE EGG WASH

1 egg, lightly beaten with
  1 tsp water

FOR THE GLAZE/DRIZZLE

30g unsalted butter

120g icing sugar

1 tsp vanilla extract

3 tsp golden rum or milk

Make the starter

- Place the milk and flour in a saucepan and stir over a medium heat with a small balloon whisk until the whisk leaves a trail on the surface and you have a thick paste. Cover with cling film unless using straight away to prevent a skin forming on the surface.

Make the dough

- Add the milk to the saucepan containing the starter and heat until small bubbles appear around the edge. Allow this to cool until it is just tepid and stir in the egg, butter and vanilla. The butter should start melting in the residual heat.

- Measure the flour, sugar, yeast and salt into the bowl of a stand mixer fitted with a dough hook. Stir to combine.

- Pour in the contents of the saucepan while mixing on low speed. You should have a shaggy, sticky dough.

- Increase the speed slightly and mix for 2–4 minutes, or until the dough becomes elastic and starts forming a ball around the dough hook.

- Stretch a small piece of dough between your fingers – if it forms a see-through membrane without tearing it is ready to use.

First rise

- Mist the bowl with oil or brush with butter. Cover loosely with greased cling film and leave to rise for 60–90 minutes (depending on the room temperature) or until doubled.

Recipe Continues Overleaf

Second rise

- Deflate the dough and tip on to a lightly floured worktop. Leave to rest for a few minutes, then roll out to form a 28x40cm rectangle. Trim the edges if needed.

- Mix together the sugar and cinnamon for the filling. Brush the dough with the melted butter and sprinkle sparingly with cinnamon sugar, allowing for a small border on the long side to your right. Press down on the sugar with your hands. You may have sugar left over.

- Roll up the dough, starting with the long edge to your left, to form a log, brushing the dough with melted butter as you roll. Pinch the edge to seal.

- Use unflavoured dental floss or a sharp serrated knife to cut the dough into ten 4cm-thick rolls.

- Place the rolls on pieces of baking paper, grouping them in two sets of four and one set of three. Brush the tops liberally with any of the leftover melted butter. Repeat with the remaining rolls.

- Cover loosley with greased cling film and leave them to rise for about 45 minutes, until doubled.

Bake

- Brush the cinnamon rolls with the egg wash. Bake in batches at 155°C for 23–25 minutes, covering with foil after 12 minutes (weigh down the foil with a wire rack). The rolls need to register over 90°C with an instant-read thermometer. Cool in the air fryer basket for 5 minutes before lifting out. Repeat with the remaining rolls.

Glaze & serve

- Place all the glaze ingredients in a saucepan and stir over a low heat until you have a pourable drizzle, adding a little water if it is too thick.

- Drizzle the glaze over the cinnamon rolls and serve.

Brioche-Baked Eggs and Ham

PREP 10 mins
AIR FRY 5-9 mins
MAKES 4

This easy breakfast of eggs, ham, cheese and brioche is so delicious and easy to throw together you will want to make it again and again.

4 brioche slices

2 tbsp butter, or as needed, softened

4 tbsp grated Parmesan

4 eggs

8 slices of ham or prosciutto, roughly torn

4 tbsp grated mozzarella

salt and pepper, to taste

- Cut a hole in each brioche slice using a 5cm round or heart-shaped cutter. Reserve the cut-out pieces. Spread butter over the bread on both sides and down the middle.

- Place a liner in the basket and add the brioche slices and cut-out pieces. You might need to bake in two batches, depending on the size of your air fryer.

- Sprinkle the bread with the grated Parmesan. Crack one egg into each of the holes.

- Tear the ham and position it on the bread, leaving the egg exposed.

- Preheat the air fryer to 180°C for 3 minutes. Cook for 5–7 minutes, or until the eggs start to set.

- Sprinkle the mozzarella over the ham, season with the salt and pepper, and cook for a further 2 minutes, or until the cheese starts to melt and bubble. Serve immediately.

NOTES

* If you like runny yolks, cook until the egg whites just start turning opaque. Take the brioche out of the air fryer and cover with a pot lid. Leave for five minutes or until the egg white has set.

* Use the recipe for Brioche on page 202.

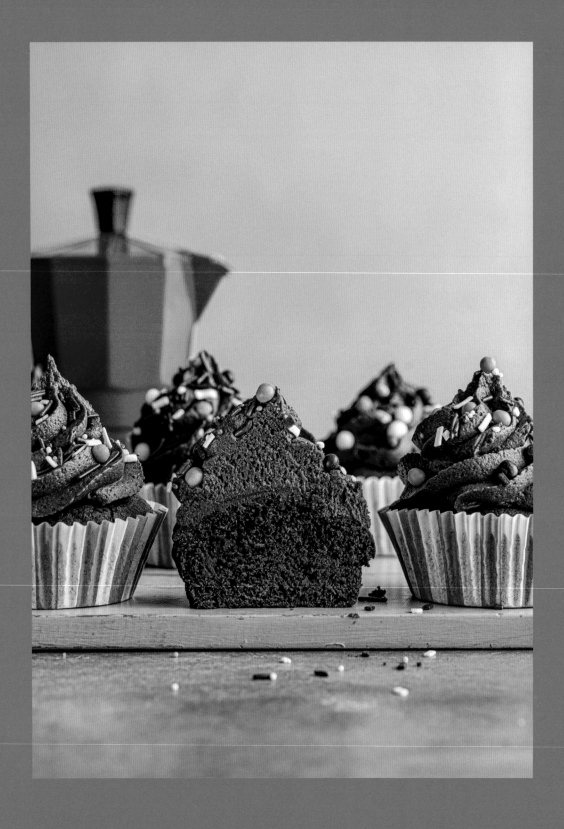

Everyday
BAKES

Lemon Drizzle Cake

A fluffy, moist lemon cake soaked with tangy lemon syrup and a crunchy sugar crust. The cake might be simple but the taste is anything but! . . . I am sure you will find yourself going back for a sneaky second slice.

FOR THE CAKE

2 unwaxed lemons, zest only
200g caster sugar
200g self-raising flour
200g unsalted butter, softened, or margarine
2 eggs
2 tbsp lemon juice

FOR THE DRIZZLE

100g granulated sugar, plus extra if needed
2 lemons, juice only

FOR THE TOPPING

lemon zest strips (optional)

- Preheat the air fryer to 160°C. Mist a 900g loaf tin with cake release and line with baking paper.

- Use a microplane to zest the lemons into your mixing bowl. Add the sugar and rub with your fingertips to release the citrus oil.

- Add all the remaining ingredients for the cake and beat together with an electric hand mixer for about a minute until the batter is completely smooth.

- Spoon the batter into the prepared tin and level. Transfer to the air fryer basket and bake for 40–45 minutes or until the cake is golden, risen and a toothpick inserted in the middle comes out clean. If the toothpick comes out with wet batter on it, continue to cook for a further 2–4 minutes before checking again. The internal temperature should be 98°C when baked.

- Remove the basket from the air fryer and leave the cake in the basket for 5 minutes. Poke holes with a skewer over the cake.

- Combine the sugar and lemon juice in a bowl and drizzle over the top. Take your time doing this so the drizzle has a chance to soak into the warm cake.

- Carefully lift the cake on to a wire rack to cool – the drizzle will set into a crunch. Decorate with lemon zest strips, if using. Keep for up to five days in a covered cake container at room temperature.

School Cake

Bite into a square of buttery nostalgia! This simple sprinkle cake is beloved by the young and the young at heart. Extremely easy to make, delicious and perfect for sharing.

FOR THE CAKE

260g self-raising flour

250g caster sugar

4 eggs

115g unsalted butter, softened, or margarine

80ml milk, semi-skimmed

1 tsp vanilla bean paste or extract

FOR THE GLAZE

140g icing sugar, sifted

1 tsp vanilla extract

½ tbsp milk, or as needed

FOR THE TOPPING

hundreds and thousands sprinkles or sprinkles of your choice

- Sift the flour and sugar into a mixing bowl. Add the eggs, butter, milk and vanilla and beat together using an electric hand mixer until the batter is completely smooth. Scrape the bottom and sides of the bowl with a spatula halfway through to make sure everything is mixed well.

- Pour the batter into a lined 20cm square cake tin and level.

- Preheat the air fryer to 150°C for 3 minutes, add the cake to the basket and bake for 35–40 minutes, or until a toothpick inserted in the middle comes out clean. The internal temperature should be 98°C.

- Lift the cake out of the tin using the paper and cool on a wire rack.

- Mix all the glaze ingredients together in a bowl until you have a thick but pourable glaze.

- Spread the glaze over the cooled cake and immediately cover with sprinkles. Leave to set before slicing.

NOTES

* A silicone cake tin allows for the cake to rise more evenly but may need an extra minute or two of cooking. A metal cake tin may cause the cake to dome slightly. If that happens, you can trim the cake until it is level.

* Store in an airtight container at room temperature for up to three days.

Vanilla Cupcakes

I know cupcakes have fallen slightly out of favour, but you can't beat a proper vanilla cupcake. These will go down a storm at kids' parties and bake sales and they are child's play to prepare.

FOR THE CUPCAKES

240g self-raising flour

1 level tbsp cornflour

½ tsp baking powder

250g caster sugar

115g margarine or softened unsalted butter

2 eggs

120ml whole milk

1 tsp lemon juice

1 tsp vanilla bean paste

FOR THE VANILLA FROSTING

260g icing sugar, sifted

140g unsalted butter, softened

80ml double cream

1 tsp vanilla bean paste or extract

sprinkles, to decorate (optional)

NOTE Place the paper cupcake cases in pudding moulds so that they keep their shape. Alternatively, use silicone cupcake cases.

Make the cupcakes

- Sift the flour, cornflour, baking powder and sugar into a mixing bowl.

- Add all the remaining cupcake ingredients to the bowl and beat together with an electric hand mixer until the batter is completely smooth. Scrape the bottom and sides of the bowl with a spatula to make sure the ingredients are well combined.

- Use a cookie scoop to divide the batter between 12 paper cupcake cases (about 55g each).

- Place the cupcakes in the air fryer basket and bake at 160°C for 18–23 minutes. You will need to bake them in batches of six.

- Check the cupcakes are risen and golden and that a toothpick inserted in the middle comes out clean. If they are not quite done, you can add a couple of minutes to the cooking time. The internal temperature should be at least 96–98°C.

- Cover the cupcakes with a tea towel for 5 minutes, then transfer to a wire rack and cool before frosting.

Make the frosting

- Put all the frosting ingredients except the sprinkles in a mixing bowl and whisk on a low speed to combine the ingredients.

- Increase the speed to medium-high and beat until the frosting holds peaks.

- Transfer to a piping bag fitted with a large star tip and pipe a generous swirl of frosting over each cupcake. Add sprinkles and serve.

Chocolate Cupcakes

PREP 10 mins
BAKE 20-23 mins
MAKES 12-14

Everybody needs a good chocolate cupcake recipe in their repertoire and this is mine. These are delicious enough on their own but transform into something special when you add a swirl of chocolate frosting and a handful of sprinkles.

FOR THE CUPCAKES

200g self-raising flour

50g cocoa powder

1 tbsp cornflour

½ tsp baking powder

250g soft light brown sugar

115g margarine or softened unsalted butter

2 eggs

120ml whole milk

1 tsp lemon juice

2 tsp vanilla bean paste

FOR THE FROSTING

260g icing sugar

30g cocoa powder

115g unsalted butter, softened

80ml double cream

1-2 tbsp hot coffee

1 tsp vanilla bean paste or extract

sprinkles, to decorate (optional)

NOTE Place the paper cupcake cases in pudding moulds so that they keep their shape. Alternatively, use silicone cupcake cases.

Make the cupcakes

- Measure the flour, cocoa powder, cornflour, baking powder and sugar into a mixing bowl. Stir well to combine and remove any lumps.

- Add the remaining cupcake ingredients and beat with a hand mixer until the batter is completely smooth. Scrape the bottom and sides of the bowl with a spatula to make sure the ingredients are well combined.

- Use a cookie scoop to divide the batter between 12–14 paper cupcake cases. Don't overfill – about two thirds full is enough.

- Place the cupcakes in the air fryer basket and bake at 160°C for 20–23 minutes. You will need to bake in batches of six.

- Check whether a toothpick inserted in the middle comes out clean. If the cupcakes are not quite done yet, add a couple of extra minutes to the cooking time.

- Transfer to a wire rack and cool before frosting.

Make the frosting

- Sift the icing sugar and cocoa powder into a mixing bowl. Add the remaining ingredients (except the sprinkles) and whisk on low speed to combine.

- Increase the speed to medium-high and beat until the frosting holds peaks. Transfer to a piping bag fitted with a large star tip.

- Pipe a generous swirl of frosting over the cupcakes, add sprinkles if you are using, and serve.

Malt Loaf

PREP 20 mins
BAKE 55–60 mins
MAKES 1 x 900g loaf

This sweet and sticky malt loaf is easy to make in one bowl. Wrap the cooled loaf in greaseproof paper and leave for a few days to allow the wonderful flavours to develop as it matures. If you can bear to wait, that is!

200g raisins/sultanas

100g dates, finely chopped

2 tsp loose-leaf Earl Grey tea
   (or the contents of
   2 teabags)

160ml water, freshly boiled

150g malt extract, plus extra
   for the top

100g dark brown sugar

2 eggs

255g plain flour

1 tsp baking powder

½ tsp bicarbonate of soda

- Grease and line a 900g loaf tin.

- Add the dried fruit and tea to a mixing bowl. Pour in the freshly boiled water, malt extract and sugar. Stir well and leave to stand for 10 minutes.

- Stir in the eggs and then sift in the flour, baking powder and bicarbonate of soda.

- Mix the batter until no streaks of flour remain and pour into the prepared tin.

- Preheat the air fryer to 160°C for 3 minutes. Bake for 55–60 minutes or until the malt loaf has risen and feels firm to the touch. A toothpick inserted in the centre should come out clean.

- Brush the warm loaf with malt extract and leave to cool in the tin.

- Wrap the loaf in two layers of greaseproof paper and store at room temperature for three to five days so the flavours can develop as the malt loaf matures.

NOTES

* If the loaf is browning too much, you can reduce the temperature by 5–10 degrees halfway through or cover with foil (but make sure the foil is secure otherwise it will fly off).

* Can also be made as two smaller loaves.

Banana Bread

PREP 10 mins
BAKE 40-45 mins
MAKES 2 small loaves

Put those unloved brown and spotty bananas to good use and make classic banana bread. A little demerara sugar on top adds some sparkle and a welcome crunch.

180g bananas (2 medium)
80ml coconut oil, melted
2 eggs
1 tsp vanilla extract
200g soft light brown sugar
250g plain flour
1½ tsp baking powder
1 tsp cinnamon
¼ tsp salt

FOR THE TOPPING
2 small bananas, peeled and
    sliced lengthwise (optional)
2 tbsp demerara sugar

- Mist two 450g loaf tins with cake release and line the sides with baking paper.

- Put the bananas, oil, eggs, vanilla and sugar into a food processor and blend until the bananas are liquidized. Pour this into a mixing bowl.

- Fold in the flour, baking powder, cinnamon and salt until no dry streaks remain.

- Divide the batter between the two loaf tins. Place the sliced banana on top and sprinkle with demerara sugar.

- Preheat the air fryer to 160°C for 5 minutes, then bake the banana bread for 40–45 minutes or until a skewer inserted in the middle comes out clean and the internal temperature is at least 98°C.

- Lift out the cake tins using the paper and cool on a wire rack.

NOTE Store in a paper towel-lined airtight container at room temperature for up to five days or wrap well and freeze for up to three months.

Lemon and Mascarpone Scones

Is there anything more heavenly than a freshly baked scone served with clotted cream and jam? Don't answer that – just go and make a batch of these fragrant air fryer delights!

zest of 1 lemon

50g caster sugar

260g self-raising flour

1 tsp baking powder

60g unsalted butter, cubed and cold

80g mascarpone, cold

1 tbsp lemon juice

1 egg

2 tbsp single cream/milk, for brushing

1 tbsp granulated sugar, to sprinkle

TO SERVE

clotted cream

strawberry jam

- Rub the lemon zest into the sugar in a mixing bowl. Stir in the self-raising flour and baking powder.

- Add the cubed butter and rub it in with your fingertips (or use a pastry cutter) until the mixture resembles chunky breadcrumbs.

- Combine the mascarpone, lemon juice and egg in a measuring jug and gradually add to the mixing bowl, stirring it in until you have a soft shaggy dough. If the dough is too dry, you can add a drop of milk until it has the right consistency.

- Tip the dough on to a lightly floured worktop and pat it into a square shape about 3½cm high. If the dough is very crumbly, use your hands to gently knead it – the warmth of your hands should help it come together.

- Cut out the scones by pressing a 6cm cutter straight down into the dough and lifting it out without twisting.

- Repeat until you have used up the dough, gathering and rerolling any scraps. Brush the top of the scones (but not the sides) with the cream/milk and sprinkle with the sugar.

- Preheat the air fryer for 5 minutes to 180°C, then place the scones on a liner in the basket, spaced apart to allow the air to circulate. Bake for 15 minutes or until the scones are well risen and golden.

- Take the scones out of the air fryer and cover with a clean tea towel for five minutes. Allow them to cool before serving with clotted cream and jam.

NOTE Avoid overworking the dough, otherwise the scones will be tough.

Carrot Cake

Carrot cake is a classic favourite, so it deserves a spot in this book. I love this slightly rustic-looking cake – it's delicious enough on its own, but the cream cheese frosting takes it to another level.

PREP 30 mins
BAKE 30-35 mins
MAKES 1 triple or double-layer cake

FOR THE CAKE
250g carrots (4 large), grated
135g crushed tinned pineapple (do not drain)
240ml light olive oil
4 eggs
350g soft light brown sugar
1 tsp vanilla extract
330g plain flour
2 tsp baking powder
1 tsp bicarbonate of soda
1 tsp ground cinnamon
1 tsp ground ginger
¼ tsp ground cloves
¼ tsp ground nutmeg
½ tsp salt
50g sweetened desiccated coconut

FOR THE FROSTING
500g icing sugar
2 tbsp cornflour
113g unsalted butter, softened
250g mascarpone cheese
2 tbsp vanilla bean paste
pinch of salt

DECORATION SUGGESTIONS
edible flowers
pecans or walnuts, roughly chopped
edible carrot decorations

Make the cake

- Mist three 15cm cake tins, or two 20cm cake tins, with cake release and line the bottoms with baking paper.

- Place the grated carrots in a large mixing bowl. Stir in the crushed pineapple, oil, eggs, sugar and vanilla. Stir vigorously to combine using a wooden spoon. Sift the flour, baking powder, bicarbonate of soda, spices and salt into the bowl. Add the coconut and stir together until the batter is well mixed. Divide the batter between the cake tins.

- Preheat the air fryer to 170°C and bake for 30–35 minutes, in batches if necessary, or until the cakes feel firm to the touch and are coming away from the edges of the tins. Leave to cool for 5 minutes. Run a knife blade around the edges of the tins and carefully invert on to a wire rack to cool completely.

Make the frosting

- Sift the icing sugar and cornflour into a bowl. Beat the softened butter and mascarpone for 5 minutes at a high speed using a hand or stand mixer. Scrape the bowl to make sure the ingredients are combined.

- Gradually add the sifted icing sugar mixture, beating it in with each addition on a medium-low speed. Add the vanilla and salt and beat until the frosting holds peaks.

Assemble the cake

- Spread the frosting over the bottom cake layer and top with the second. Repeat if you have baked three layers.

- Cover the whole cake with a thin layer of frosting and smooth using a scraper. Pipe any remaining frosting over the top. Decorate with edible flowers, nuts or edible carrot decorations just before serving.

Marble Cake

Marble Cake was my mum's 'everyday cake' and she made it often for me and my brother. This is my slightly tweaked version of her recipe and it's just as delicious as I remember. You can play around to create different flavour combinations if you like.

PREP 20 mins
BAKE 60-70 mins
MAKES 1 x 900g loaf

FOR THE CAKE
230g self-raising flour
250g caster sugar
1 tsp baking powder
80ml buttermilk
4 eggs
115g margarine

FOR THE CHOCOLATE BATTER
2 tbsp cocoa powder, sifted
zest of an orange
2 drops orange extract

FOR THE VANILLA BATTER
1 tbsp self-raising flour, sifted
2 tsp vanilla bean paste

FOR THE CHOCOLATE GLAZE (OPTIONAL)
175g dark chocolate chips
125ml double cream
1 tbsp golden syrup

FOR THE TOPPING
orange zest strips (optional)

- Mist a 900g loaf tin with cake release and line the bottom and sides with baking paper, letting the paper hang over the sides. Clip the paper down.

- Combine the flour, sugar and baking powder in a bowl.

- Add the buttermilk, eggs and margarine. Beat using a hand or stand mixer until you have a smooth batter, scraping the bottom and sides of the bowl as needed.

- Place half the batter in a separate bowl. Add the cocoa powder, orange zest and extract and stir vigorously to combine. Add the flour and vanilla to the original bowl and mix in.

- Transfer the chocolate batter to a piping bag and the vanilla batter to another. Pipe straight lines of the batter into the prepared tin, alternating between chocolate and vanilla.

- Draw a chopstick through the batter to create a marbled effect.

- Preheat the air fryer to 160°C for 3 minutes, then place the tin in the basket. Bake for 60–70 minutes, or until a skewer inserted in the centre comes out clean and the cake feels firm to the touch. If the cake is not quite done, add 5 minutes to the cooking time or as needed.

- Lift the cake out of the tin using the overhanging paper and allow to cool on a wire rack. Place the chocolate chips in a bowl.

- Heat the cream and golden syrup in a saucepan until little bubbles appear around the edge. Pour over the chocolate and leave for 2 minutes.

- Stir until the chocolate has melted and you have a smooth glossy glaze. Drizzle over the cake, smoothing with an offset spatula if needed. Decorate with orange zest strips, if using. Allow the glaze to set before slicing.

Cookies
AND BARS

Chocolate Chip Cookies

PREP 10 mins
BAKE 15–17 mins
MAKES 12–15

These moreish Chocolate Chip Cookies magically disappear practically the minute they leave the air fryer basket. You can also make one giant cookie using this recipe and serve it topped with vanilla ice cream for dessert. Beware . . . seriously addictive.

150g soft light brown sugar

90g unsalted butter, at room temperature

1 egg

1 tsp vanilla extract

150g plain flour

½ tsp salt

½ tsp baking powder

½ tsp bicarbonate of soda

½ tsp cinnamon

pinch of ground nutmeg (optional)

90g porridge oats

100g large chocolate chips, plus extra to top

- Beat the sugar and butter in a stand mixer fitted with a paddle attachment (or use a hand mixer).

- Add the egg and vanilla and beat to combine, scraping the sides of the bowl as needed.

- Add the flour, salt, baking powder, bicarbonate of soda, cinnamon and nutmeg if using. Beat to combine or mix everything together with a spoon. Beat in the oats, then use a wooden spoon to fold in the chocolate chips.

- Line the air fryer with a liner or baking paper (make sure it is weighed down). Form four balls of cookie dough (approx. 2 tbsp each) and place into the air fryer basket spaced apart. Press a few extra chocolate chips on top of the cookie dough.

- Bake for 15–17 minutes at 160°C or until the cookies are browning at the edges. Check at the 12-minute mark.

- Take the basket out of the air fryer and leave the cookies in the basket for 2–3 minutes to firm up before transferring to a wire rack to cool.

- Repeat with the remaining cookie dough or keep in the fridge for another day. Alternatively, freeze the cookies on a tray prior to baking and cook straight from frozen, adding a couple of minutes to the cooking time.

To make a giant cookie

- Press the cookie dough into a lined 20cm springform cake tin. Bake for 30–35 minutes, checking at the 25-minute mark. The edges should be cooked but the middle can be a little soft and squidgy. Cool before serving – the cookie will get firmer.

NOTE Slightly underbaked cookies are very tasty but need to cool before transferring out of the air fryer otherwise they will fall apart.

Apple Pecan Blondies

PREP 10 mins
BAKE 40 mins
MAKES 16 squares

The scent of these apple blondies is simply out of this world! Luckily they taste just as amazing and are the perfect treat with a cup of coffee or tea.

FOR THE APPLES

180g peeled and diced
apple (2 apples)
2 tbsp soft light brown sugar
2 tbsp unsalted butter,
cubed
2 tsp cinnamon
pinch of salt

FOR THE BLONDIES

200g soft light brown sugar
115g unsalted butter,
softened, or margarine
1 egg
1 tsp vanilla extract
180g plain flour
½ tsp baking powder
½ tsp bicarbonate of soda
¼ tsp salt
50g pecans, chopped

FOR THE TOPPING

30g pecans, chopped
2 tbsp demerara sugar
2 tbsp butterscotch fudge,
finely chopped

- Place the apple, sugar, butter, cinnamon and salt in a small bowl. Cook for 10 minutes at 180°C in the air fryer, stirring halfway through. The apples should be tender but not mushy. Set aside to cool.

- Beat the sugar and butter until pale and creamy.

- Add the egg and vanilla and beat until mixed in.

- Add the flour, baking powder, bicarbonate of soda and salt and beat together until you have a soft cookie dough. Fold in the chopped pecans.

- Transfer three quarters of the dough into a greased and lined 20cm square dish. Scatter over the apple mix and dot the remaining dough over the top.

- Sprinkle with the pecans, sugar and fudge pieces and bake at 180°C for 20 minutes, then lower the heat to 160°C and bake for a further 10 minutes.

- Lift the dish out of the air fryer basket and allow the blondies to cool completely before slicing.

NOTES Store in a paper towel-lined airtight container at room temperature for up to three days.

Shortbread Fingers

PREP 10 mins
CHILL 30 mins
BAKE 10-13 mins
MAKES 24-30

Crumbly, buttery and irresistible shortbread cookies flavoured with Earl Grey tea and orange zest – these are the perfect treat with your cup of tea and great for sharing.

zest of 1 orange

contents of 1 Earl Grey teabag

125g caster sugar

225g unsalted butter, softened

1 tsp vanilla extract

300g plain flour

50g rice flour

1 tbsp cornflour

¼ tsp baking powder

¼ tsp salt

1 tbsp orange juice, or as needed

icing sugar, as needed, plus extra for dusting and rolling

1–2 tbsp granulated sugar (optional)

TO DECORATE

150g white chocolate, melted

fruit powder or sprinkles (optional)

FOR THE CHOCOLATE DIP

150g white chocolate chips, melted

fruit powder or sprinkles to decorate (optional)

- Place the zest, tea and sugar in a mixing bowl. Rub the mix with your fingertips to release the citrus oil in the zest.

- Add the softened butter and vanilla and beat together until creamy using a hand or stand mixer. Use a spatula to scrape the bottom and sides of the bowl as needed.

- Combine the flour, rice flour, cornflour, baking powder and salt in a separate bowl.

- Gradually add this to the mixing bowl and beat on a low speed until incorporated. Add the orange juice if the mixture is too dry.

- Tip the dough on to a large piece of cling film and gather into a ball. The mixture will be quite crumbly, but the warmth of your hands will help to bring it together.

- Wrap the dough in the cling film and chill in the fridge for at least 30 minutes.

- Dust a work surface with icing sugar. Cut the dough into three sections and roll out to 3mm thick in batches. Cut into 1cm wide by 10cm long fingers and dock with a fork.

- Place the cookies on a silicone or paper liner. Preheat the air fryer to 150°C for 3 minutes and bake in batches for 10–13 minutes, or until the edges start to colour.

- Sprinkle with the granulated sugar if using. Allow the cookies to rest for 2 minutes in the air fryer basket before carefully transferring to a wire rack to cool.

NOTES

* Dip the cookies in the melted white chocolate and place on greaseproof paper. Sprinkle with fruit powder or sprinkles before the chocolate sets.

* Store in an airtight container for up to a week.

Cinnamon Cookies

PREP 15 mins
BAKE 9 mins
MAKES 20+

These fragrant cinnamon cookies have such a delightful crunch! Leave them plain or make them into sandwich cookies filled with Biscoff spread.

130g unsalted butter, softened, or margarine
225g soft light brown sugar
1 egg, beaten
2 tbsp honey
300g plain flour, plus extra for rolling
2 tbsp wheatgerm
2 tsp cinnamon
⅛ tsp ground cloves
⅛ tsp ground cardamom
pinch of salt
pinch of baking powder

FOR THE FILLING (OPTIONAL)
smooth Biscoff spread, as needed

- Beat the butter and sugar together until light and creamy using a stand mixer or a hand mixer. Stop the mixer and scrape down the sides of the bowl midway through. Gradually add the beaten egg and honey and beat until well incorporated.

- Add the flour, wheatgerm, spices, salt and baking powder and briefly beat together until just combined – do not overbeat or the cookies will be tough. You can use a spatula to fold everything together if you prefer.

- Tip the dough on to a lightly floured worktop and gather into a ball. Flatten to form a disc, wrap in cling film and chill for at least 30 minutes.

- Lightly dust your worktop and rolling pin with flour. Roll out the dough to 3mm thick and cut shapes using floured cookie cutters.

- Preheat the air fryer to 170°C. Add an air fryer paper liner to the air fryer basket and add the cookies, spacing slightly apart. (Make sure the paper liner is weighed down at the edges with the cookies.)

- Bake for 9 minutes in batches, until the cookies are just starting to colour at the edges. Transfer to a wire rack to cool.

- These can be filled with smooth Biscoff spread to make about 20 sandwich cookies.

- Store in an airtight container for up to a week at room temperature. Filled cookies will keep for 3-4 days.

Flapjacks

PREP 10 mins
BAKE 40 mins
MAKES 12-14

These vegan and gluten-free flapjacks are packed with nuts, seeds and dried fruit, making them just a smidge healthier and even more delicious. Grab one for an on-the-go breakfast or pack in lunchboxes for an afternoon treat.

200g vegan butter, cubed

150g soft light brown sugar

150g golden syrup

1 tbsp maple syrup

3 tbsp almond butter (smooth)

1 tsp vanilla extract

zest of 1 orange

320g porridge oats

30g ground almonds

100g whole almonds, roughly chopped

100g dried cranberries, chopped

50g mixed seeds (sunflower, pumpkin, linseed, sesame)

1 tsp cinnamon

pinch of salt

- Place the vegan butter, sugar, golden syrup, maple syrup, almond butter, vanilla and orange zest in a saucepan. Stir over a low heat until the vegan butter has melted, the sugar has dissolved and the mixture is smooth. Do not boil.

- Measure the oats, ground almonds, chopped almonds, cranberries, mixed seeds, cinnamon and salt into a mixing bowl and stir to combine.

- Pour the liquid ingredients into the dry and stir well to combine.

- Press the flapjack mix into a greased and lined 20cm square tin. Make sure it is tightly packed and level. Score the top where you want to cut it later.

- Preheat the air fryer to 160°C for 3 minutes, add the tin to the basket and bake for 40 minutes, covering the tin with foil after 15 minutes, or until golden, firm on top and crispy at the edges.

- Lift the flapjacks out of the tin and transfer to a wire rack to cool.

- Cut along the scored lines and store in an airtight container at room temperature for up to five days or in the fridge for up to a week.

NOTES

* Instead of almonds you can use peanuts or cashews and replace the almond butter with smooth peanut butter.

* To freeze flapjacks, separate each slice with strips of greaseproof paper and freeze in an airtight container.

Millionaire's Peanut Butter Shortbread

PREP 20 mins
BAKE 35-40 mins
CHILL 2+ hrs
MAKES 16 squares

The combination of chocolate, caramel and peanut butter makes this incredibly rich Millionaire's Peanut Butter Shortbread absolutely irresistible! Cut into small squares and share responsibly.

FOR THE SHORTBREAD LAYER

200g plain flour
1 tbsp cornflour
100g caster sugar
¼ tsp salt
170g unsalted butter, cubed

FOR THE CARAMEL LAYER

395g tin of caramel
100g soft light brown sugar
100g unsalted butter, cubed
70g smooth peanut butter
generous pinch of salt

FOR THE CHOCOLATE LAYER

200g dark chocolate chips
50g milk chocolate chips
1 tbsp unsalted butter

FOR THE PEANUT BUTTER DRIZZLE

3 tbsp smooth peanut butter
2 tsp unsalted butter

Make the shortbread

- Mist a 20cm square tin with cake release and line the bottom and sides with baking paper.

- Put the flour, cornflour, sugar and salt in a food processor and pulse briefly to combine. Add the cubed butter and pulse in short bursts until the mix resembles breadcrumbs.

- Press the shortbread into the tin until it's packed down and level. Dock the surface with a fork.

- Preheat the air fryer to 160°C. Add the cake tin to the air fryer basket and bake for 35–40 minutes or until the shortbread is a light golden colour. Cool completely in the tin.

Make the caramel

- Place the caramel, sugar, butter, peanut butter and salt in a saucepan. Cook over a medium heat, stirring constantly, until the butter has melted.

- Bring the mix to a simmer over a low heat and cook for 7–10 minutes, stirring gently. The caramel should register just over 110°C.

- Pour the caramel over the shortbread layer and chill in the fridge until it sets.

COOKIES AND BARS

74

Recipe Continues Overleaf
• • • •

Make the topping

- Put the chocolate chips and butter in a bowl and microwave for short bursts until the chocolate starts to melt. Stir until it is completely smooth.

- Pour the melted chocolate over the caramel and level using a small offset spatula.

- Place the peanut butter and butter in a small saucepan and stir until melted. Then transfer to a small sandwich bag and snip a hole in one corner.

- Drizzle the peanut butter over the chocolate in four or five straight lines.

- Give your tin a half turn and lightly draw a chopstick through the peanut butter lines to create a marbled effect.

- Chill in the fridge for at least two hours or until completely set.

Slice & serve

- Lift the shortbread out of the tin with the baking paper. Run a large knife under hot water and wipe dry. Push this firmly through the shortbread to slice it, wiping the knife between cuts.

- Keep in the fridge and consume within a week.

Berry Crumble Bars

PREP 30 mins
BAKE 55 mins
CHILL 8+ hrs
MAKES 16 squares

Let's bake these buttery and crumbly bars of berry goodness! The tart filling contrasts beautifully with the golden crunchy topping, making these the perfect afternoon treat. You can use any combination of berries you like – I usually grab frozen berries intended for smoothies as they are cheaper than fresh fruit.

FOR THE BERRY FILLING

600g mixed berries, frozen
1 tbsp lemon juice
1 tbsp seedless raspberry or strawberry jam
1 tsp vanilla extract
2½ tbsp cornflour

FOR THE BASE

113g unsalted butter, softened
175g caster sugar
2 eggs
½ tsp almond extract
200g plain flour
1 tsp baking powder
½ tsp bicarbonate of soda
pinch of salt

FOR THE CRUMBLE TOPPING

220g plain flour
50g soft light brown sugar
50g granulated sugar
1 tsp ground cinnamon
1 tsp baking powder
pinch of salt
113g unsalted butter, cubed
2 tbsp demerara sugar

Prepare the filling

- Put the berries in a saucepan – no need to thaw them. Add all the remaining filling ingredients and bring to the boil.
- Reduce the heat to a simmer and cook until the berries have started to burst and the filling is thick and glossy. Cool before using, ideally by chilling in the fridge for a few hours or overnight.

Make the base

- Mist a 20cm square springform cake tin with cake release and line the bottom with baking paper.
- Cream the butter and sugar with a stand or hand mixer until light and fluffy.
- Beat in the eggs and almond extract until well combined.
- Sift in the flour, baking powder, bicarbonate of soda and salt. Beat until just combined.
- Spread the batter in the prepared tin with an offset spatula.
- Preheat the air fryer to 160°C for 3 minutes. Place the cake tin in the basket and bake for 15–20 minutes, or until golden.

Prepare the crumble

- Combine the flour, sugars, cinnamon, baking powder and salt in a bowl.
- Rub in the butter until the mixture is crumbly and holds together if pinched.

Recipe Continues Overleaf

Add the filling & topping

- Spread the filling over the base and cover with the crumble topping. Sprinkle with the demerara sugar.

- Bake for 30 minutes or until the crumble is golden and the filling starts to bubble up through the sides.

Slice & enjoy

- Cool completely, ideally by chilling overnight in the fridge to make sure the filling has set.

- Run a knife around the edges of the cake tin and release the springform. Use a large serrated knife to slice into squares, wiping the blade in between each cut.

- Store in the fridge in an airtight container for up to five days.

NOTES

* Make sure the filling is jammy and thick, otherwise it will soften the base too much and not set properly.

* If the topping is getting too dark, you can cover it with foil, clipping on the edges of the tin or weighing it down.

* Store any leftover berries in the freezer until you have enough to use for the filling.

Jam Tarts

PREP 20-30 mins
CHILL 1 hr
BAKE 24-26 mins
MAKES 3, 6-8 servings per tart

These jam tarts are my version of a Greek recipe called *Pasta Flora*, which closely resembles the Austrian *Linzer Torte*. Whatever the origin and name, they are delicious! Just be patient and wait for the tarts to cool before slicing …

FOR THE DOUGH

100g ground almonds
120g icing sugar
225g unsalted butter, softened
1 egg
1 tbsp freshly squeezed orange juice, sieved
1 tsp vanilla bean paste
½ tsp salt
½ tsp ground cinnamon
¼ tsp ground cardamom
330g plain flour
icing sugar as needed, for dusting and rolling

FOR THE TOPPING

1 egg yolk
1 tbsp milk
2 tbsp sanding or granulated sugar

FOR THE FILLING

160–200g seedless strawberry jam, or jam of your choice

Prepare the dough

- Pulse the ground almonds, flour and icing sugar in a food processor to combine or sift both ingredients into a bowl. This will help remove any lumps.

- Place the butter in a mixing bowl or the bowl of your stand mixer. Beat until the butter is creamy, scraping the bottom and sides of the bowl as needed.

- Add a spoonful of the almond and sugar mixture, and the egg, orange juice and vanilla. Beat to combine, then gradually add the remaining dry ingredients.

- Tip the dough on to a large piece of cling film and form into a disc. Wrap tightly and rest in the fridge for at least 1 hour or overnight.

Make the tarts

- Divide the dough in half and keep any you are not using wrapped and chilled.

- Dust your worktop with icing sugar. Roll out the dough until it is 6mm thick (a rolling pin with spacing discs is ideal for this purpose).

- Use a 16cm tart ring (or the top of a springform cake tin) to cut out three discs. Transfer the discs to a baking liner and lightly dock with a fork without piercing all the way through. If you can, transfer to a baking tray and chill the dough in the fridge.

- Roll out the rest of the dough and use a pastry wheel to cut 1cm wide strips. Alternatively, roll the pastry into a 18cm disk and cut out shapes using small cookie cutters to use as the jam tart lid. Press down and crimp edges to seal and trim any excess pastry.

Recipe Continues Overleaf

- Spoon jam over the rolled-out tart bases, leaving a small border around the edge.

- Lightly whisk the egg yolk and milk in a small bowl. Brush the edge of the tarts with the egg wash.

- Arrange the strips over the tart base in a trellis pattern and press down the edges to seal. Trim any excess dough, gather into a ball and roll it out again. Alternatively, top with the tart lid.

- Brush the pastry strips with egg wash and sprinkle with the sugar. You will need to bake the tarts in batches. Carefully transfer the first tart to a wire rack.

- Preheat the air fryer to 150°C for 3 minutes. Place the wire rack in the air fryer basket and bake for 24–26 minutes. If the tart is colouring too quickly, you may need to reduce the temperature to 145°C.

- Allow the tart to cool before slicing and serving. Store in a paper towel-lined airtight container for three to four days.

NOTES

* You can also use this dough to make sandwich cookies. Use Linzer cookie cutters to cut out the cookies and sandwich them together with jam or curd.
* Bake in batches at 145–150°C for 8–9 minutes, or until the cookies start colouring at the edges. Transfer to a wire rack to cool.
* Dust the cookies with icing sugar. Spread the rest with jam and sandwich together.
* Store in an airtight tin for three to four days. The filling will eventually cause the cookies to soften so they won't keep for longer than that. Unfilled cookies can be stored for up to a week.

Macarons

Macarons are delicate, oh-so-pretty and delicious. They are also a bit of a challenge, whether you are a novice or an experienced baker, so don't get discouraged if they don't look picture-perfect – they'll taste just as good.

PREP 30 mins
DRY 30-40 mins
BAKE 18-20 mins
MAKES 20-25

GLUTEN-FREE

FOR THE SHELLS
150g ground almonds
150g icing sugar
120ml egg whites from a
   carton
150g caster sugar
few drops vanilla extract
few drops food colouring
   gel (optional)

FOR THE FILLING
150g dark chocolate chips
120ml double cream
30g unsalted butter
2 tbsp golden syrup

Make the shells

- Put the ground almonds and icing sugar in a food processor and pulse a few times until combined. Sift the mixture into a large bowl, discarding anything that won't go through the sieve.

- Add 60ml of the egg whites to the bowl and mix vigorously with a silicone spatula until you have a smooth paste.

- Put the caster sugar, remaining egg whites, vanilla and food colouring, if using, in the bowl of your stand mixer. Place the bowl over a saucepan of barely simmering water (the bottom of the bowl should not come into contact with the water). Stir the egg whites mixture with a balloon whisk for a few minutes until the sugar dissolves. Use a finger to test whether the sugar has dissolved.

- Fit the bowl to your stand mixer and whisk on maximum speed until you have a glossy meringue that forms peaks.

- Add a third of the meringue to the bowl with the almond paste and mix it together with a silicone spatula to loosen.

- Fold in the remaining meringue with your spatula, using a large circular motion, scraping the bottom and sides of the bowl as you fold. Mix until the batter flows slowly like molten lava. Take care not to overmix the batter.

- Transfer the macaron mix into a large piping bag fitted with a plain round tip.

- Use 20cm square silicone baking mats or reusable baking liners. Hold the bag vertically over the mat and pipe the macarons, spaced slightly apart, using a quick circular motion as you stop squeezing the bag.

- Lift the mat off the worktop and drop back down to release air bubbles.

Recipe Continues Overleaf

- If the macarons have little 'peaks' pat them down with a clean wet finger. Leave the macarons to dry until the shells lose their shine and become touch dry.

- Preheat the air fryer to 100–110°C. Bake for 18–20 minutes or until the macarons have a smooth dry top and are firm to the touch. Allow the macarons to dry for at least 10 minutes before peeling off the mat.

Fill the macarons

- Put the chocolate chips, cream, butter and golden syrup in a bowl. Microwave for 30-second bursts, stirring in between until the chocolate melts. Cool before using and transfer to a piping bag fitted with a small round tip.

- Pipe the chocolate filling on half the shells, allowing space for it to expand, and then sandwich the shells gently together.

- Store in an airtight container and consume within two days (the shells will soften once filled).

NOTES

* You can use the egg whites left over from making the Apple Hand Pie dough on page 157.

* The trickiest aspect to macarons is knowing when to stop mixing the batter. If you mix it too vigorously or for too long it will become very free-flowing, causing it to spread too much when piping. It's best to undermix it until you get more confident.

4

Holiday
BAKES

Hot Cross Bun Loaf

PREP 30 mins
PROVE 3+ hrs
BAKE 40-45 mins
MAKES 1 x 900g loaf

Don't let the long list of ingredients intimidate you – this Hot Cross Bun Loaf is well worth the effort! Soft, fluffy and delicious, it makes excellent toast for an Easter breakfast, although if it were up to me, I would serve it year-round.

FOR THE DRIED FRUIT
100g mixed dried fruit
50g citrus peel
boiling water, as needed

FOR THE STARTER
20g bread flour (2 level tbsp)
120ml whole milk

FOR THE DOUGH
80ml whole milk
40ml fresh orange juice
1 egg
55g unsalted butter, cubed
360g bread flour, plus extra
   for dusting
80g soft light brown sugar
2 tsp rapid-rise yeast
1 tsp mixed spice
½ tsp salt
1 orange, zest only
1 lemon, zest only

FOR THE EGG WASH
1 egg, lightly beaten

FOR THE CROSS
2 tbsp whole milk
2 tbsp plain flour, or as
   needed

TO GLAZE
2-3 tbsp smooth apricot
   jam

Soak the fruit

- Place the dried fruit and citrus peel in a small bowl and pour in boiling water to just cover. Allow the fruit to rehydrate, draining any excess liquid before using.

Make the starter

- Place the flour and milk in a saucepan and stir over a medium heat with a small balloon whisk until the whisk leaves a trail on the surface and you have a thick paste. Cover with cling film unless using straight away to prevent a skin forming on the surface.

Make the dough

- Add the milk to the saucepan containing the starter and heat until small bubbles appear around the edge.

- Allow this to cool until it is just tepid, then stir in the orange juice, egg and butter. Leave to stand until the butter starts to melt and stir to combine.

- Place the flour, sugar, yeast, spice, salt and zest in the bowl of a stand mixer fitted with a dough hook. Stir to combine.

- Pour in the contents of the saucepan while mixing on a low speed. You should have a shaggy, sticky dough.

- Increase the speed slightly and knead for 2–4 minutes, or until the dough becomes elastic and starts forming a ball around the dough hook. If the dough is very sticky, add a little more flour, a tablespoon at a time. Stretch a small piece of dough between your fingers – if it forms a see-through membrane without tearing, it is ready to prove.

First rise

- Mist the bowl with oil. Cover with greased cling film and leave to rise until doubled, 60–90 minutes.

Shape & second rise

- Deflate the dough and tip on to a lightly floured worktop. Leave to rest for a few minutes, then stretch the dough out to form a large rectangle.

- Scatter some of the dried fruit over the dough and fold the edges inwards to encase the filling. Continue until you have used all the dried fruit, kneading the dough so that it is evenly dispersed.

- Divide the dough into four equal portions. Flatten each to form a rectangle, then roll the long edge to make a small Swiss roll shape. Repeat with the rest of the pieces.

- Mist a 900g loaf tin with cake release and line the sides with baking paper. Place the rolls in the loaf tin. Push any fruit that's on the surface into the dough or pick them off as they can burn.

- Cover the tin loosely with cling film and allow to rise for 45 minutes.

Bake

- Brush the loaf with the egg wash.

- Combine the milk and flour for the cross in a bowl until you have a smooth, thick but pourable paste. Place this in a sandwich bag and snip a small hole in one corner.

- Use the bag to pipe a cross over each of the loaf sections.

- Preheat the air fryer to 200°C for 5 minutes. Reduce the temperature to 160°C and place the loaf tin in the basket. Bake for 40–45 minutes, or until the loaf is a deep brown colour and the internal temperature is 92–94°C. Brush the warm loaf with the jam to glaze.

- Cool before slicing. It is delicious served toasted with butter.

NOTE Slice and freeze for up to three months. Toast from frozen and serve.

Simnel Cake

PREP 20 mins
BAKE 1–1¼ hrs
SERVES 12

Simnel cake has a long history – it was traditionally given by servant girls to their mothers for Mothering Sunday, also known as Simnel Day. These days it is associated with Easter and often decorated with eleven marzipan balls, one for each of the Apostles minus Judas. I have added one for Jesus to make it twelve, if only so everyone gets one on their slice!

FOR THE DRIED FRUIT
250g mixed dried fruit
1 tbsp boiling water
1 orange, zest and juice
1 tbsp self-raising flour

FOR THE CAKE
200g self-raising flour
250g soft light brown sugar
60g ground almonds
1 tsp mixed spice
1 tsp baking powder
4 eggs
115g margarine
80ml buttermilk
½ tsp almond extract
½ tsp vanilla extract
3 tbsp flaked almonds

TO DECORATE
120g golden marzipan
3 tbsp smooth apricot jam

- Mist a 20cm square springform cake tin with cake release and line the bottom with baking paper.

- Place the mixed dried fruit in a bowl and add the water and orange zest and juice. Leave for 20 minutes to allow the fruit to plump up slightly. Drain any excess liquid before using and toss with the flour.

- Place the flour, sugar, almonds, mixed spice and baking powder in a bowl and stir to combine.

- Add the eggs, margarine, buttermilk and extracts and beat using a hand or stand mixer until the batter is smooth. Use a spatula to scrape the bottom and sides of the bowl as needed.

- Fold in the dried fruit and transfer the batter to the prepared tin. Scatter the flaked almonds on top.

- Preheat the air fryer to 160°C for 3 minutes. Place the cake tin in the basket and bake for 1 hour or until a toothpick comes out clean.

- Divide the marzipan into twelve pieces and roll each into a small ball.

- Leave the cake in the tin and brush with the apricot jam. Position the marzipan balls on top of the cake, spacing them out evenly. Use a blowtorch to lightly brown the top of the marzipan balls for a few seconds if you like.

- Cool for 10 minutes, then run a knife blade around the edges of the tin. Release the cake on to a wire rack to cool before slicing.

NOTE The cake can be stored in an airtight container for three to four days.

Red Velvet Halloween Cake

PREP 20 mins
BAKE 70-85 mins
SERVES 10-12

Transform a towering red velvet layer cake into a ghoulish showstopper topped with meringue bones and a splattering of edible 'blood'. Be assured it tastes incredible – there will be no crumbs left at the end of your Halloween party!

FOR THE EDIBLE BLOOD

80ml cranberry juice

2 tbsp cornflour

240g golden syrup

1 tsp vanilla extract

1 tsp red food colour paste, or as needed

FOR THE MERINGUE BONES

120ml egg whites from a carton

240g caster sugar

½ tsp cream of tartar

1 tsp vanilla paste

FOR THE CAKE

180ml buttermilk

2 tsp red food colour paste, or as needed

1 tbsp red wine vinegar

2 tsp bicarbonate of soda

1 tsp vanilla bean paste or vanilla extract

300g caster sugar

200g unsalted butter, softened, or margarine

3 eggs

2 tbsp cocoa powder

320g plain flour

¼ tsp salt

Make the edible blood

- Combine the juice and cornflour in a saucepan. Add the golden syrup and vanilla and bring to a simmer, stirring, until the mix thickens.

- Take off the heat and add the red food colouring to create the desired shade. Transfer to a jar and cool before using.

Make the meringue bones

- Combine the egg whites, sugar, cream of tartar and vanilla in the bowl of your stand mixer. Place the bowl over a saucepan of simmering water (the water should not touch the bowl). Stir over a low heat until the sugar dissolves.

- Fit the bowl to the stand mixer with the whisk attachment. Whisk on maximum speed until you have a glossy and stiff meringue that holds firm peaks. Transfer the meringue to a piping bag fitted with a plain round tip.

- Cut a piece of baking paper that fits the air fryer basket. Place it in the basket and pipe the bones, spacing them slightly apart. Pipe slightly different shapes and lengths so that you can use the bones to cover the sides of the cake or to pile on top. You will need to bake these in batches, so it is best to prepare these a day ahead.

- Bake at 100°C for 30–40 minutes or until they are dry and lift off the paper easily. Store in an airtight container until needed.

Recipe Continues Overleaf

FOR THE BUTTERCREAM

250g unsalted butter, softened

395g sweetened condensed milk

2 tsp vanilla extract

⅛ tsp salt

Prepare the cake

- Combine the buttermilk and food colouring in a large mixing bowl, adding as much colouring as needed to achieve the perfect blood-red colour. Stir in the red wine vinegar and bicarbonate of soda.

- Add the vanilla, sugar, softened butter and eggs and beat with a hand mixer (or stand mixer) to combine.

- Sift in the cocoa powder, flour and salt, then beat together until you have a smooth batter.

- Divide the batter between three greased and lined 15cm cake tins. Preheat the air fryer to 160°C and bake in batches for 40–45 minutes, or until the cakes are risen, springy to the touch and a toothpick inserted in the middle comes out clean. You can check the progress of the cakes as they bake, to see whether they are done faster than the cooking time allows or to decrease the heat setting if they are colouring too much.

- Cool in the tins for 5 minutes, then carefully turn out on to a wire rack. Allow the cakes to cool completely before frosting.

Prepare the buttercream

- Beat the butter until light and fluffy, then gradually add the condensed milk, beating well. Add the vanilla and salt and beat on the maximum speed setting until the buttercream is smooth and holds peaks.

- Transfer to a piping bag fitted with a plain round tip.

Assemble the Halloween cake

- Level the cake layers as needed, saving any scraps to blitz in a food processor to make the cake topping.

- Pipe a generous layer of buttercream to sandwich the cake layers together. Smooth a layer of buttercream over the cake. Top the cake with the crumbs, if using.

- Stick the bones on the cake, securing them with buttercream if needed, breaking some in half to fit. Drizzle with edible blood and serve immediately.

NOTES

* Make sure to use bake-stable paste or gel food colouring. If you can, use colouring labelled 'Red Velvet', which is created specifically for this cake and will give it a really vibrant red colour.

* The edible blood and cake layers can be made a day ahead. The meringue bones can be made ahead as well and stored in an airtight container.

* Only add the decorations when you are ready to serve the cake. They will eventually melt due to the moisture.

Pumpkin Rolls

These adorable rolls are not just shaped like mini pumpkins, they contain pumpkin purée and wonderful warming spices. They're irresistible served warm and spread with butter, and the perfect side dish for soups and stews.

FOR THE STARTER
120ml whole milk
20g bread flour (2 level tbsp)

FOR THE DOUGH
120ml whole milk
1 egg
55g unsalted butter, softened
50g pumpkin purée
350g bread flour, plus extra for dusting as needed
1 tbsp caster sugar
1 tsp salt
2 tsp rapid-rise yeast
pinch of freshly grated nutmeg
pinch of mixed spice

FOR THE EGG WASH
1 egg beaten with a splash milk

FOR THE TOPPING (OPTIONAL)
poppy or sesame seeds
cinnamon sticks or pretzels, for the stalks

Make the starter

- Place the milk and flour in a saucepan and stir over a medium heat with a small balloon whisk until the whisk leaves a trail on the surface and you have a thick paste. Cover with cling film unless using straight away to prevent a skin forming on the surface.

Make the dough

- Add the milk to the saucepan containing the starter and heat until small bubbles appear around the edge. Allow this to cool until it is just tepid and stir in the egg, butter and pumpkin purée. The butter should start melting in the residual heat.

- Measure the flour, sugar, salt, yeast and spices into the bowl of a stand mixer fitted with a dough hook. Stir to combine.

- Pour in the contents of the saucepan while mixing on a low speed. You should have a shaggy, sticky dough.

- Increase the speed slightly and mix for 2–4 minutes, or until the dough becomes elastic and starts forming a ball around the dough hook. If the dough is very sticky, add a little more flour, a tablespoon at a time.

- Stretch a small piece of dough between your fingers – if it forms a see-through membrane without tearing, it is ready to use.

First rise

- Mist the bowl with oil. Cover with greased cling film and leave to rise for 60–90 minutes (depending on room temperature) or until doubled.

Recipe Continues Overleaf

Shape/second rise

- Deflate the dough and tip on to a lightly floured worktop. Leave to rest for a few minutes then divide into eight pieces of equal weight to make eight rolls.

- Flatten each piece into a disc. Fold the edges inwards to form a ball. Flip over and roll in the palm of your hand to form a smooth ball. Repeat with the remaining pieces to form eight rolls.

- Cut four pieces of string into 30cm pieces. Dip the string in vegetable oil and run between your fingers to get rid of excess oil.

- Arrange in a criss-cross pattern on your worktop. Place the first roll in the middle of the strings and brush with egg wash.

- Tie the strings (not too tightly, to allow for the bread to expand as it bakes) over the roll so that it is divided into eight equal sections. Cut any excess string. Repeat this with the rest of the rolls.

- Add a greased liner to the air fryer basket and mist the basket sides with cooking spray. Place the rolls in the basket, spaced slightly apart.

- Cover with a clean towel and set aside for 45 minutes or until doubled, puffy and touching each other.

Bake

- Brush the bread rolls with the egg wash and sprinkle with any toppings if using. Air fry for 25 minutes at 160°C. Flip them over and bake for a couple more minutes to brown them.

- Remove the string before serving. Add small pieces of cinnamon sticks or pretzels to create the pumpkin stalks.

NOTE Store in an airtight container for up to three days and reheat them in the air fryer for a few minutes before serving.

Pumpkin Pie

PREP 20 mins
BAKE 45-50 mins
SERVES 10-12

This is NOT your usual pumpkin pie! Filo pastry is baked first until golden and crisp, then covered with pumpkin custard filling and baked again until it sets. Serve warm with a light drizzle of maple syrup.

FOR THE PASTRY
150g unsalted butter, melted
7 sheets filo pastry

FOR THE FILLING
400g sweetened
  condensed milk
100g pumpkin purée, tinned
2 eggs
1 tbsp maple syrup
1 tsp vanilla extract
2 tsp mixed spice
1 tsp ground cinnamon
¼ tsp ground nutmeg
¼ tsp salt

TO TOP
20g pecans, roughly
  chopped
1 tbsp granulated sugar
maple syrup, to serve

- Line a 20cm springform cake tin with baking paper and brush with melted butter.

- Take the pastry out of the fridge and allow it to come to room temperature for 10 minutes. Keep the filo covered with a damp tea towel to prevent it from drying out.

- Lay one sheet of pastry on your worktop with the long side facing you. Brush with melted butter and cover with a second sheet.

- Brush with melted butter and loosely fold into a concertina shape, starting with the edge closest to you. Roll into a snail shape and place in the middle of the prepared tin.

- Repeat the brushing and folding of the filo, arranging the pastry around the central coil. You should have enough to fill the cake tin. Make sure the pastry has room to expand as it bakes.

- Preheat the air fryer to 160°C. Place the tin in the basket and bake for 20 minutes, or until the pastry is crisp and golden.

- Combine all the filling ingredients in a bowl, then pour over the cooked filo, encouraging it to seep into all the folds. Sprinkle with the pecans and sugar.

- Bake for another 25–30 minutes or until the custard is set. Cool slightly before releasing from the tin. Serve warm with a drizzle of maple syrup.

Festive Fruitcake

PREP 15 mins
BAKE 55-60 mins
SERVES 8-10

The easiest Christmas fruitcake you will ever bake . . . and one of the tastiest.
Prepare three to four weeks prior to serving to allow the cake to mature.

FOR THE CAKE

500g dried mixed fruit
75ml hot tea (made with two
  black teabags)
75ml brandy, rum or port
200g sweetened
  condensed milk
125g self-raising flour
2 level tbsp ground almonds
1 tsp mixed spice
1 tsp bicarbonate of soda
zest of 1 orange

FOR FEEDING THE CAKE

brandy, as needed

FOR THE TOPPING

4 tbsp smooth apricot jam,
  to glaze, or as needed
500g golden marzipan
icing sugar for rolling, as
  needed

FOR THE ROYAL ICING

60ml egg whites from a
  carton
450g icing sugar
1 tbsp lemon juice
1 tsp liquid glucose

Prepare the cake tin

- Mist a 17cm springform tin with cake release and line the bottom with baking paper. Line the sides of the tin with two strips of baking paper, letting the paper reach ½cm above the rim. Secure the paper with small clips.

Make the cake batter

- Add the fruit to a mixing bowl and pour in the hot tea. Allow the fruit to soak for an hour or until plump. You can microwave for 30 seconds to speed this up. Stir in the brandy and condensed milk.

- Add the flour, almonds, mixed spice, bicarbonate of soda and orange zest and stir well until no dry streaks remain.

Bake

- Transfer the cake batter into the prepared tin and level. Preheat the air fryer for 3 minutes at 150°C, then place the cake tin in the basket and bake for 55–60 minutes or until the internal temperature of the cake is 98°C.

Store & feed

- Lift the cake out of the air fryer basket and allow to cool completely. Pierce the top of the cake with a skewer and drizzle with a little brandy.

- Release from the springform tin, leaving the lining on the cake. Wrap with two layers of baking paper and then a layer of foil.

- Drizzle the cake with a little brandy once a week for three to four weeks or up to three months, wrapping it back up afterwards.

Recipe Continues Overleaf

**DECORATION IDEAS
(OPTIONAL)**

Gingerbread Cookies
  (see page 108)
blanched almonds
glacé cherries

Decorate (optional)

- Flip the cake over so the flat underside is now on top. Heat the jam in a saucepan and brush the entire cake. Use small pieces of marzipan to fill any small holes on the cake surface.

- Dust your worktop liberally with icing sugar and soften the marzipan in your hands. Roll out the marzipan to a circle of about 25cm.

- Position the marzipan circle over the cake and press down so that it sticks. Smooth the top and sides, trim any excess marzipan and leave it to dry for a few hours or overnight.

Make the royal icing

- Beat the egg whites until frothy, then gradually add the icing sugar a tablespoon at a time, mixing on a low speed with a hand or stand mixer.

- Add the lemon juice and liquid glucose and beat on the high-speed setting until the icing forms firm peaks. (Cover the surface of the icing with cling film to prevent it from drying out unless you are using it straight away.)

Finishing touches

- Spoon the royal icing over the marzipan and spread using an offset spatula so that it resembles small snowy peaks. Leave to dry so that it hardens and decorate with blanched almonds and glacé cherries or iced Gingerbread Cookies.

NOTE This cake doesn't contain any eggs so it can be made vegan by using vegan sweetened condensed milk and skipping the icing.

Gingerbread House Cake

PREP 15 mins
BAKE 35-40 mins
ASSEMBLE 20 mins
SERVES 9

This rustic gingerbread house is, in fact, a gingerbread layer cake with cinnamon cream cheese frosting. It's adorably cute and delicious in equal measure and a great way to involve little kids – get them to help you decorate!

DRY INGREDIENTS

185g plain flour

185g soft light brown sugar

2 tsp baking powder

½ tsp bicarbonate of soda

2 tsp ground ginger

1 tsp ground cinnamon

¼ tsp ground cloves

¼ tsp salt

WET INGREDIENTS

100g unsalted butter, cold
  and cubed

2 eggs

2 tbsp treacle

1 tsp vanilla extract

85ml whole milk

15ml fresh orange juice

1 tsp orange zest

FOR THE FROSTING

250g mascarpone

113g unsalted butter,
  softened

2 tsp vanilla bean paste

480g icing sugar

1 tbsp cornflour

1 tsp ground cinnamon

pinch of salt

Make the cake

- Sift all the dry ingredients into a mixing bowl or the bowl of your stand mixer. Add the cold cubed butter and beat on a low speed until the mixture resembles wet sand.

- Combine the eggs, treacle, vanilla, milk, orange juice and orange zest in a measuring jug. Pour into the mixing bowl and mix until the batter is completely smooth, scraping the bowl as needed.

- Pour the batter into a greased and lined 20cm square springform cake tin. Place in the air fryer basket and bake for 35–40 minutes at 160°C or until a skewer inserted in the centre comes out clean.

- Cool in the cake tin and then release on to a wire rack to cool.

Make the frosting

- Place the mascarpone, butter and vanilla in a mixing bowl or the bowl of a stand mixer. Beat until light and fluffy, scraping the bowl a few times.

- Sift the icing sugar, cornflour, cinnamon and salt into a bowl. Add this to the mascarpone/butter mixture a few tablespoons at a time and beat on a low-speed setting until combined.

- Increase the speed to maximum and beat for 3–4 minutes until the frosting holds peaks. Place in the fridge unless you are using it immediately.

Recipe Continues Overleaf

DECORATION SUGGESTIONS

chocolate fingers, pretzels
  or Mikado sticks, to cover
  the house
chocolate or plain
  Shreddies, for the roof
Oreo cookies
chocolate wafers
icing sugar, for dusting

Assemble the cake

- Trim the cake edges to create a perfectly square cake. Use a cake leveller or knife to slice the cake in half horizontally. Slice each half into two equal pieces vertically so you now have four rectangular layers. Use a ruler for accuracy.

- Smear a little frosting on a rectangular board or platter to secure the cake. Place the bottom cake layer on a board or platter and spread with frosting. Top with the second layer and repeat until the cake forms the main body of a house three layers tall.

- Slice the final layer into two pieces vertically for the roof, one 7cm wide and the other 3cm wide. Position the wider piece in the middle of the assembled cake and cover with frosting.

- Top with the narrow layer and build the sides with frosting to create the roof. Smooth a generous layer of frosting over the entire gingerbread house.

Decorate

- Use the chocolate fingers, pretzels or Mikado sticks to cover the front and side of the house, cutting them to size as needed. Leave some space for windows and a door. Use the plain end of the Mikado sticks or pretzel sticks to create the door, or see Notes.

- Stick Shreddies on the roof to create a thatched-style roof. Dust with icing sugar and serve.

NOTES

* You can use Gingerbread Cookies to create the windows and door if you like (see page 108).

* You can prepare the cake a couple of days ahead of assembling to give it a chance to firm up. Wrap it in cling film and keep it at room temperature.

Gingerbread Cookies

PREP 10 mins
BAKE 8-9 mins
MAKES 12+

These delicious gingerbread cookies are so easy to make and perfect for decorating. Put on some Christmas tunes, pull on that sparkly sweater and get your bake on!

50g soft light brown sugar

70g golden syrup

30g treacle

60g unsalted butter

1 tsp mixed spice

1 tsp cinnamon

1 tsp ground ginger

pinch of ground cloves

1 tsp bicarbonate of soda

1 egg

280–300g plain flour, plus extra for dusting and rolling

FOR THE ROYAL ICING

30ml egg whites from a carton

225g icing sugar, sifted

1 tbsp lemon juice

- Place the sugar, golden syrup, treacle, butter and spices in a mixing bowl and microwave for 30–40 seconds until the butter melts. Alternatively, do this in a saucepan over low heat. Set aside to cool.

- Stir in the bicarbonate of soda and the egg. (Take care the bowl is not too hot otherwise the egg will scramble.) Gradually stir in the flour, adding as much as needed to create a pliable dough that's the consistency of play dough. Form into a ball and cover with cling film. Rest for 10 minutes.

- Lightly dust your worktop with flour. Roll out the dough in batches using a rolling pin. Cut out the cookies using your favourite festive cutters and place on a paper liner set over a wire rack, spaced slightly apart.

- Bake in batches in a preheated air fryer for 8–9 minutes until the cookies start browning at the edges. Carefully lift on to a wire rack and leave to cool.

- To make the royal icing, beat the egg whites until frothy, then gradually add the icing sugar a tablespoon at a time, mixing on a low speed with a hand or stand mixer. Add the lemon juice and beat on a high-speed setting until the icing holds firm peaks. (*Cover the surface with cling film to prevent it from drying out unless you are using it straight away.*)

- Place the icing in a silicone piping bottle and decorate the cookies, allowing the icing to dry before moving them to an airtight container.

NOTE To make stained-glass gingerbread cookies, cut out a small window shape in the cookies and place on a greased liner. Place a brightly coloured hard-boiled sweet in the space and bake as above. Let the cookies cool completely before lifting off the paper (to allow for the sweet centre to cool down).

Mince Pies

PREP 20 mins
CHILL 30+ mins
BAKE 12-14 mins
MAKES 12-14

I love home-made mince pies and these adorable air fryer mince pies are delicious and easy to make – no tin required. The pastry is buttery yet crisp – the perfect partner for the sweet filling.

FOR THE PASTRY

230g plain flour

50g icing sugar, plus extra for rolling and dusting

pinch of salt

125g cold unsalted butter, cubed

2 egg yolks

2 tbsp double cream

1 tsp vanilla extract

FOR THE FILLING

250g mincemeat, stirred

FOR THE EGG WASH

1 egg yolk, lightly beaten

Prepare the pastry

- Sift the flour, icing sugar and salt into a mixing bowl. Add the butter and beat on a low speed until the mixture resembles breadcrumbs.

- Combine the egg yolks, double cream and vanilla in a measuring jug. Add to the mixing bowl and beat together very briefly to combine.

- Line your worktop with cling film. Tip the pastry crumbs on to it and use the cling film to gather the pastry together, kneading with your hands as needed to form a disc. Chill the pastry for at least 30 minutes or overnight before using.

Make the mince pies

- Cut the pastry in half, keeping any you are not using straight away in the fridge covered with cling film.

- Dust your worktop with icing sugar and roll out the pastry to a thickness of 3mm. Cut out circles using a 7.5cm fluted pastry cutter. Cut a small hole out of half the circles – these will be our pastry lids.

- Place about half a tablespoon of mincemeat in the middle of a pastry circle and brush the edges with the egg yolk. Top with a pastry lid and press down to seal. You can crimp the edges with your fingertips or a fork. Brush with the egg wash.

- Repeat until you have used up all the mincemeat and pastry, gathering any scraps and rolling out as needed.

- Preheat the air fryer to 180°C. Place a liner in the air fryer basket and carefully transfer the mince pies to it, spacing them slightly apart. Bake in batches of six for 12–14 minutes, or until the mince pies are beautifully golden and the filling is bubbling. Cool on a wire rack, dust with icing sugar and serve.

NOTES

* Reduce the temperature by 5–10° if the mince pies are browning too quickly.

* You can use home-made or store-bought mincemeat. Jazz up store-bought mincemeat by adding orange zest and a splash of brandy.

Honey Spice Cookies

PREP 10 mins
BAKE 25 mins
MAKES 12

Melomakarona are as popular in Greece where I grew up as mince pies are in the UK. Every house will bake batches of these fragrant honey-soaked cookies throughout the festive season to eat and gift to others. One bite takes me straight back to my childhood, helping my mum bake these.

FOR THE SYRUP

125ml water

125g granulated sugar

150g honey or golden syrup

1 cinnamon stick

1 piece orange peel

FOR THE COOKIES

60ml light olive oil

60g unsalted butter or
vegan baking spread

60g caster sugar

2 tbsp freshly squeezed
orange juice

2 tbsp brandy

1 tbsp orange zest

½ tsp baking powder

½ tsp bicarbonate of soda

1 tsp ground cinnamon

⅛ tsp ground cloves

⅛ tsp ground nutmeg

½ tsp salt

250g plain flour

FOR THE TOPPING

60g walnuts, finely chopped

NOTE Use vegan butter and replace the honey in the syrup with agave or golden syrup to make a vegan version of this recipe.

Make the syrup

- Put all the syrup ingredients in a large saucepan, stir together, then bring to the boil. Reduce the heat to a low simmer and cook, stirring, for 5–10 minutes, or until slightly thickened. Skim any foam that forms on top of the syrup. Discard the cinnamon stick and orange peel.

Prepare the cookies

- Put the oil, butter and sugar in a bowl and beat together for 5 minutes using a hand mixer or a stand mixer fitted with the paddle attachment.

- Combine the orange juice, brandy, orange zest, baking powder, bicarbonate of soda, spices and salt in a measuring jug. Add to the mixing bowl and beat on medium to combine.

- Gradually add the flour until the dough forms a ball and is pliable and not sticky. Roll the dough into a thin log and cut into twelve equal pieces. Roll each into ball, then press them against a box grater to create a pattern – the cookies will now be an oval shape.

- Preheat the air fryer to 170°C. Place the cookies on a piece of baking paper and transfer to the air fryer basket, spaced slightly apart. Bake, in batches, for 20–25 minutes until evenly coloured and firm.

Soak in the syrup

- Remove from the air fryer and immediately place in the syrup, flipping them over to coat them fully. Repeat until all the cookies have been soaked.

- Layer the cookies on a platter, spoon any remaining syrup over them and sprinkle with the chopped nuts. Keep at room temperature, in an airtight container, for up to a month.

5

Celebration
CAKES

Classic Victoria Sponge

PREP 15 mins
BAKE 50-55 mins
SERVES 10

You can't have afternoon tea without a glorious Victoria Sponge taking pride of place on the table! This cake is deceptively simple but the combination of a soft butter-rich sponge with buttercream and jam is truly fit for a queen.

FOR THE CAKE

250g self-raising flour
1 tbsp cornflour
250g caster sugar
½ tsp baking powder
120ml whole milk
2 tsp vanilla bean paste
3 eggs
115g margarine or softened
  unsalted butter

FOR THE VANILLA BUTTERCREAM

260g icing sugar, sifted
115g unsalted butter,
  softened
80ml double cream
1 tsp vanilla bean paste or
  extract

FOR THE FILLING & DECORATING

5 tbsp seedless raspberry or
  strawberry jam, to fill
handful fresh strawberries or
  raspberries, to decorate
icing sugar, for dusting

- Mist a 20cm cake tin with cake release and line the bottom with baking paper.

- Sift the flour, cornflour, sugar and baking powder into a mixing bowl.

- Add all the remaining cake ingredients and beat with a hand mixer until the batter is completely smooth. Scrape the bottom and sides of the bowl with a spatula to make sure the ingredients are well combined.

- Spoon the batter into the prepared cake tin and level it. Place the tin in the air fryer basket and bake at 160°C for 30 minutes. Reduce the temperature to 150°C and bake for a further 20 minutes, or until the cake is risen, golden and a toothpick inserted in the middle comes out clean. If it is not done yet, add 4–5 minutes to the cooking time.

- Cool for 5 minutes in the tin. Then run a knife blade around the edges of the tin and carefully turn the cake out on to a wire rack to cool completely.

- Use a cake leveller to slice the cake into two.

NOTES

* Alternatively, you could divide the batter between two 18cm silicone cake pans and bake as instructed above.

* Cover the cake with foil after 30 minutes if it is browning too much.

Recipe Continues Overleaf
• • •

- Put all the frosting ingredients in a mixing bowl and whisk on a low speed to combine them. Increase the speed to medium-high and beat until the frosting holds peaks.

- Transfer the frosting to a piping bag fitted with a round tip and pipe frosting over the bottom cake layer and spoon the jam over it.

- Cover with the second cake layer, pressing it down lightly. Pipe any remaining frosting on top.

- Add the berries, dust with icing sugar and serve.

NOTE This cake has an annoying habit of looking perfectly baked but still being slightly doughy in the middle. Check with an instant-read thermometer that it is 98°C before taking it out. Store in the fridge for up to two days.

Coffee & Walnut Cake

PREP 15 mins
BAKE 30-35 mins
SERVES 8-10

This old-fashioned coffee and walnut cake is a doddle to make yet tastes absolutely decadent. The rustic coffee and ground walnut sponge sandwiched with delicious espresso buttercream keeps well for nearly a week – not that it ever lasts that long!

100ml whole milk, plus 1 tbsp
   lemon juice
50g walnuts
1 tbsp instant espresso
   powder (can use decaf)
165g plain flour
165g soft light brown sugar
2 tsp baking powder
½ tsp bicarbonate of soda
¼ tsp salt
100g cold unsalted butter,
   cubed
2 eggs
1 tsp vanilla paste

FOR THE BUTTERCREAM
2–3 tbsp instant espresso
   powder (can use decaf)
½ tbsp hot water
500g icing sugar
160g unsalted butter,
   softened
50ml double cream

TO DECORATE
walnut halves or chocolate-
   covered espresso beans

- Mist two 18cm cake tins with cake release and line the bottoms with baking paper.

- Combine milk and lemon juice in a measuring jug and leave for a few minutes – the milk will curdle.

- Put the walnuts and coffee powder in a mini chopper or food processor and pulse until finely ground.

- Place the flour, sugar, ground walnuts, baking powder, bicarbonate of soda and salt into a mixing bowl and stir well to combine.

- Add the cubed butter and beat with a hand mixer until the mixture resembles breadcrumbs.

- Add the eggs, curdled milk and vanilla and beat together until the batter is smooth, scraping the bowl with a spatula as needed.

- Preheat the air fryer to 170°C. Divide the batter into the prepared cake tins and bake for 30–35 minutes one at a time. Check whether the cake needs to be covered with foil after 15 minutes.

- The cakes are ready when they are springy to the touch and a skewer inserted in the centre comes out clean.

- Turn the cakes out of the tins and cool on a wire rack before frosting.

Make the buttercream

- Dissolve the espresso powder in the water. Put the icing sugar, butter and coffee in a stand mixer. Start mixing on the lowest speed setting to avoid an icing-sugar snowstorm.

- Once the ingredients are roughly combined, increase to the maximum speed setting and whisk for 4–5 minutes until the frosting is light and fluffy. Add the double cream and continue to beat together until incorporated.

Recipe Continues Overleaf
• • •

Assemble the cake

- Place the bottom cake layer on a plate and add a generous layer of frosting. Sandwich together with the second cake layer and cover the entire cake with a thin layer of frosting. Chill the cake for 20 minutes.

- Add a generous layer of frosting over the sides of the cake and smooth or swirl using a palette knife.

- Put any remaining buttercream in a piping bag fitted with a star tip and pipe a pattern around the perimeter of the cake.

- Decorate with walnut halves or chocolate-covered espresso beans.

NOTE Store the cake in an airtight container at room temperature for up to five days.

Fresh Strawberry Cake

This cake is bursting with fresh strawberry flavour, from the soft and fluffy sponge to the irresistible frosting. The freeze-dried strawberry powder brings such intense flavour to the frosting, you'll swear you're biting into juicy fresh strawberries.

FOR THE CAKE

350g plain flour

330g caster sugar

1 tbsp baking powder

½ tbsp bicarbonate of soda

3 eggs

200g unsalted butter, softened and cubed

180g full-fat strawberry yogurt

2 tsp vanilla bean paste

FOR THE FROSTING

420g icing sugar

30g freeze-dried strawberry powder

230g unsalted butter, softened and cubed

60ml double cream

2 tsp vanilla bean paste

pinch of salt

WHITE CHOCOLATE DRIP (OPTIONAL)

90g white chocolate chips

40ml double cream

TO DECORATE

10 fresh strawberries

Make the cake

- Mist three 15cm silicone cake tins with cake release and line the bottoms with baking paper.

- Place the flour, sugar, baking powder and bicarbonate of soda in a mixing bowl. Stir to combine.

- Add the eggs, butter, yogurt and vanilla bean paste to the bowl and beat together using a hand or stand mixer until the batter is smooth, scraping the bowl halfway through.

- Divide the batter between the prepared cake tins and level.

- Preheat the air fryer to 160°C for 3 minutes. Bake, in batches, for 35–40 minutes or until the cake is springy to the touch and a toothpick inserted in the centre comes out clean.

- Cool in the tins for 5 minutes, then run a thin knife blade around the edges of the tins. Gently invert the cakes on to a wire rack to cool.

Prepare the frosting

- Sift the icing sugar and strawberry powder into a bowl and set aside.

- Cream the butter on a high speed using a hand mixer or a stand mixer fitted with the paddle attachment. Beat for at least 5 minutes, stopping to scrape the bottom and sides of the bowl with a spatula as needed. The butter needs to be creamy and smooth.

- Decrease the speed to low and gradually add the icing sugar mixture, waiting until each addition is incorporated before adding more.

CELEBRATION CAKES

123

Recipe Continues Overleaf
• • •

- Add the cream, vanilla and salt and beat on a low speed until the frosting is completely smooth and holds peaks.

- Transfer the frosting to a piping bag fitted with a large star tip.

Make the white chocolate drip

- Place the white chocolate chips in a bowl.

- Stir the cream in a saucepan over a low heat until small bubbles start forming around the edge of the pan.

- Take the cream off the heat and pour over the chocolate. Leave to stand for 2 minutes, then gently stir until the chocolate has completely melted and the mixture is smooth. Cool for 5–10 minutes before using.

Assemble the cake

- Add a dot of frosting to a cake board the same size as your cake and place the first cake layer on top.

- Pipe a layer of frosting over the first layer and level with an angled offset spatula. Press down lightly so the cake sticks to the frosting.

- Position the second cake layer on top and repeat.

- Place the final cake layer on top, bottom side up. Press down lightly.

- Spread a layer of frosting over the entire cake using the angled offset spatula. Use a cake scraper to smooth the frosting (a cake turntable is useful at this stage).

- Put the white chocolate drip in a sandwich bag and snip a small hole in one corner. Drizzle around the edge of the cake, letting it drip prettily down the sides.

- Pipe any remaining frosting over the top of the cake.

- Decorate with whole and halved strawberries just before serving.

Ultimate Chocolate Cake

PREP 15 mins
BAKE 35-40 mins
SERVES 10-12

This chocolate cake is always requested by my children on their birthdays. It's a deliciously rich and moist cake, especially when sandwiched with the world's most decadent chocolate frosting. But want to know the best part? It is ridiculously easy to make.

FOR THE CAKE

300g plain flour

60g cocoa powder

330g soft light brown sugar

1 tbsp instant espresso powder (optional)

1 tbsp baking powder

½ tbsp bicarbonate of soda

½ tsp salt

200g unsalted butter

3 eggs

200ml buttermilk

2 tsp vanilla extract

FOR THE CHOCOLATE FROSTING

175g dark chocolate chips, melted and cooled

260g icing sugar

6 tbsp cocoa powder

150g unsalted butter, softened

120ml whole milk

DECORATION SUGGESTIONS

sprinkles, chocolate shavings

Make the cake

- Mist two 20cm cake tins with cake release and line the bottoms with baking paper.

- Sift the flour, cocoa powder, sugar, espresso powder (if using), baking powder, bicarbonate of soda and salt into a large bowl.

- Add the butter, eggs, buttermilk and vanilla to the flour mix. Using a hand or stand mixer, beat on the lowest speed setting until the ingredients start to come together. Then increase the speed gradually, until the batter is completely smooth. Stop the mixer and scrape the sides and bottom of the bowl to make sure everything is well mixed.

- Divide the batter between the prepared tins and level.

- Preheat the air fryer to 160°C and bake, one at a time, for 35–40 minutes.

- Check the cake is baked by inserting a toothpick in the centre – it should come out clean and the cake should feel springy to the touch.

- Cool the cake in the tins for 5 minutes. Run a knife around the edge of the tins and gently invert on to a wire rack. Cool the cake layers completely before frosting.

Make the chocolate frosting

- Put the chocolate chips in a bowl and melt in the microwave in 30-second bursts, stirring in between until they melt. Alternatively, set the bowl over a pot of simmering water and allow it to melt gradually. Set the chocolate aside to cool before using.

Recipe Continues Overleaf
• • •

- Sift the icing sugar and cocoa powder into a mixing bowl or the bowl of your stand mixer.

- Add the softened butter and start mixing on a low speed, gradually adding the milk until the frosting is well combined.

- Add the melted chocolate to the mix and beat until the frosting holds soft peaks.

- Transfer to a large piping bag fitted with a large star tip.

Assemble the cake

- Pipe a generous layer of frosting over the bottom cake layer and top with the second.

- Cover the entire cake with the frosting, smoothing it with a scraper or swirling it with an offset spatula.

- Pipe any leftover frosting on top of the cake and add sprinkles or any other decorations before serving.

- Slice the cake using a serrated knife, wiping the knife clean between each slice.

NOTES

* The cake layers can be baked up to two days ahead and kept at room temperature covered with cling film.
* The frosted cake keeps well for several days in a covered container at room temperature away from direct sunlight.

Very Vanilla Cake

PREP 15 mins
BAKE 35-40 mins
SERVES 10-12

There's nothing basic about this fragrant vanilla cake. It's the easiest cake you will ever make, with a soft buttery crumb and an intense vanilla flavour. Sandwich and frost with my velvety buttercream and you have a fabulous cake that stays lovely and fresh for days.

FOR THE CAKE

360g plain flour
330g caster sugar
1 tbsp cornflour
1 tbsp baking powder
½ tbsp bicarbonate of soda
½ tsp salt
200g unsalted butter or
  margarine
3 eggs
200ml buttermilk
2 tsp vanilla extract

FOR THE VANILLA FROSTING

250g unsalted butter,
  softened
460g icing sugar, sifted
2 tsp vanilla bean paste
3 tbsp double cream
pinch of salt

DECORATION SUGGESTIONS

sprinkles, meringue cookies,
  edible flowers

Make the cake

- Mist two 20cm cake tins with cake release and line the bottoms with baking paper.

- Sift the flour, sugar, cornflour, baking powder, bicarbonate of soda and salt into a large bowl or the bowl of your stand mixer.

- Add the butter, eggs, buttermilk and vanilla.

- Using a hand or stand mixer, beat on the lowest speed setting until the ingredients start to come together. Increase the speed gradually, until the batter is completely smooth. Stop the mixer and scrape the sides and bottom of the bowl to make sure everything is well mixed.

- Divide the batter between the prepared tins and level.

- Preheat the air fryer to 160°C and bake, one at a time, for 35–40 minutes.

- Check each cake is done by inserting a toothpick in the centre – it should come out clean and the cake should feel springy to the touch.

- Cool each cake in the tin for 5 minutes. Run a knife around the edge and gently invert on to a wire rack. Cool the cake layers completely before frosting.

Make the vanilla frosting

- Put the butter in the bowl of your stand mixer fitted with the paddle attachment or use a hand mixer. Beat on a high speed for 5–7 minutes, using a spatula to scrape the sides and bottom of the bowl as needed. You want the butter to be incredibly creamy and light in colour.

- Gradually add the sifted icing sugar, beating in well with each addition until it is mixed in.

CELEBRATION CAKES
129

Recipe Continues Overleaf
● ● ●

- Add the vanilla, double cream and salt. Beat on a medium-high speed until the frosting is completely smooth and holds peaks. Chill in the fridge unless you are using it immediately.

- Transfer to a large piping bag fitted with a large star tip.

Assemble the cake

- Pipe a layer of frosting on the bottom cake layer and top with the second.

- Cover the entire cake with the frosting, smoothing it with a scraper or swirling it with an offset spatula.

- Pipe any leftover frosting on top of the cake and add sprinkles or any other decorations before serving.

- Slice the cake using a serrated knife, wiping the knife clean between each slice.

NOTES

* The cake layers can be baked up to two days ahead and kept at room temperature covered with cling film.

* The frosted cake keeps well for several days in a covered container at room temperature away from direct sunlight.

* The vanilla buttercream will be a creamy off-white due to the butter content. If you want a bright white buttercream, add a tiny amount of violet food colouring or adjust the colour using white colouring paste.

* You can tint the vanilla buttercream any colour you like by adding food colouring gels or paste.

Cookie Butter Cake

Lovers of Biscoff will be thrilled with this cookie butter cake. It's so easy to make and absolutely delicious, whether you are serving it at a birthday party or simply as a treat.

FOR THE CAKE

225g self-raising flour

225g soft light brown sugar

1½ tsp baking powder

225g margarine or softened unsalted butter

4 eggs, room temperature

2 tbsp semi-skimmed milk

3 tbsp smooth Biscoff spread

1 tsp vanilla extract

FOR THE BISCOFF BUTTERCREAM

250g unsalted butter, softened

395g can sweetened condensed milk

2 tbsp smooth Biscoff spread

1 tsp vanilla bean paste

large pinch of salt

TO DECORATE

2 tbsp smooth Biscoff spread, warm, to drizzle

2 tbsp white chocolate curls (optional)

1 tbsp Biscoff cookie crumbs (optional)

Make the cake

- Mist a deep 20cm baking tin with cake release and line the bottom with baking paper or a reusable liner.

- Add the flour, sugar and baking powder to a mixing bowl and stir to combine. Make sure the sugar doesn't have any lumps.

- Add the rest of the cake ingredients to the bowl and beat together using a hand or stand mixer until the batter is smooth. Use a spatula to wipe the sides and bottom of your bowl as needed.

- Transfer the batter to the cake tin and level. Preheat the air fryer to 160°C for 3 minutes. Put the cake tin into the air fryer basket and air fry for 30 minutes. Lower the temperature to 150°C and bake for a further 25 minutes or until a tester comes out clean.

- If the cake still feels wobbly in the middle, add 5-10 minutes to the cooking time. Remove the cake from the air fryer and let it stand for 5 minutes before turning out on to a wire rack.

Make the buttercream

- Place the butter in a large bowl and cream for 5–7 minutes until it is pale and fluffy, scraping the bowl as needed.

- Gradually add the condensed milk, while beating on a medium speed. Increase the speed to maximum once it has all been added and beat until the buttercream is silky, smooth and holds peaks. Add the Biscoff, vanilla and salt and beat it in.

- Transfer the buttercream to a piping bag fitted with a Russian tip or large star tip.

Recipe Continues Overleaf

Assemble the cake

- Slice the cake in half using a cake leveller or a large serrated knife.

- Pipe a generous amount of frosting over the bottom cake layer and top with the second. Spread a thin layer of frosting over the top of the cake, smoothing it flat.

- Drizzle the Biscoff spread around the edge of the cake, letting it drip down the sides. Pipe any remaining buttercream on top of the cake.

- Sprinkle with the white chocolate curls or cookie crumbs if using. Slice and enjoy!

NOTE Store the cake in a covered container at room temperature for up to three days.

Passion Fruit Tres Leches Cake

PREP 20 mins
BAKE 35-40 mins
SERVES 12-16

This is an absolute delight. A simple vanilla sponge is transformed into a sensational dessert by soaking it in three types of milk. The tartness of the passion fruit cuts through the sweetness and adds a tropical note.

FOR THE PASSION FRUIT SYRUP

8 large passion fruits
3 tbsp caster sugar

FOR THE CAKE

4 eggs
200g caster sugar
2 tsp vanilla extract
70ml whole milk
30ml passion fruit juice
   (leftover from the syrup)
190g plain flour
10g cornflour
1 tsp baking powder

FOR THE MILK SOAK

250ml evaporated milk
200ml sweetened
   condensed milk
2 tbsp double cream
1 tsp vanilla extract

FOR THE TOPPING

250ml double cream, cold
4 tbsp icing sugar
1 tsp vanilla bean paste

Make the syrup

- Slice seven of the passion fruits in half and scoop out the seeds and pulp into the bowl of a mini chopper or blender. Pulse a few times to separate the juice and pulp from the seeds.

- Strain the mixture through a fine sieve to extract the passion fruit juice. Set aside 30ml of the juice to use in the cake. Store the remainder in a jar in the fridge.

Prepare the cake

- Separate the eggs, placing the egg whites in one bowl and the yolks in another. Add 150g of the caster sugar to the egg whites and place the bowl over a saucepan of simmering water.

- Use a balloon whisk to stir the egg whites for a few minutes until the sugar dissolves. Whisk the egg white mixture with a hand mixer until you have a glossy meringue.

- Add the remaining caster sugar and vanilla to the bowl of the egg yolks and whisk at high speed until pale and frothy. Stir in the milk and passion fruit juice. Sift the flour, cornflour and baking powder into the bowl and stir to combine until no dry streaks remain.

- Gradually add the meringue, folding it in gently so as not to knock the air out.

- Transfer the batter into a greased 20cm square baking dish.

- Place the dish in the basket of your air fryer and bake for 35–40 minutes at 160°C. The cake is ready when a skewer inserted in the centre comes out clean.

Recipe Continues Overleaf
• • •

Add the milk soak & chill

- Combine the evaporated milk, condensed milk, double cream and vanilla in a measuring jug.

- Poke holes over the entire cake using a skewer and spoon about half the milk mixture over the top. Leave for 5–10 minutes to absorb. Repeat once more – you will probably not need all the milk soak. Store any leftover liquid in a jar in the fridge to serve alongside the cake.

- Allow the cake to cool before covering with foil and placing it in the fridge for a few hours or overnight.

Top with whipped cream & serve

- Whisk the double cream, icing sugar and vanilla together on medium speed until you have peaks.

- Spread a thick layer of the cream over the entire cake. Pipe any remaining cream over the top to decorate if you like.

- Scoop the pulp and seeds from the last remaining passion fruit and add to a saucepan along with the reserved passion fruit juice and sugar. Stir over a low heat for a few minutes until the sugar dissolves. The syrup will thicken as it cools.

- Drizzle the cake with the passion fruit syrup and serve with the remaining milk on the side.

Very Berry Chocolate Cake

PREP 30 mins
BAKE 30-35 mins
SERVES 10-12

This deliciously rich vegan chocolate cake is so easy to make and a great option for those avoiding eggs and dairy. Transform the cake into a showstopper for special occasions by covering it with a medley of fresh berries.

FOR THE CAKE

120g coconut oil, melted

240ml oat milk, or your choice of vegan milk

80ml hot water

2 tbsp red wine vinegar

2 tsp vanilla extract

230g plain flour

230g brown sugar

100g cocoa powder

2 tsp bicarbonate of soda

½ tsp salt

FROSTING & FILLING

400g icing sugar

60g cocoa powder

250g vegan butter, softened

60ml oat milk, warm

2 tsp vanilla extract

4 tbsp berry conserve (optional)

TO DECORATE

200g strawberries

200g blueberries

200g raspberries

100g blackberries

Make the cake

- Mist three 15cm cake tins with cake release and line the bottoms with baking paper.

- Combine the coconut oil, oat milk, hot water, vinegar and vanilla in a large mixing bowl.

- Sift the flour, sugar, cocoa powder, bicarbonate of soda and salt into the bowl and stir to combine until you have a glossy batter.

- Preheat the air fryer for 3 minutes at 150°C.

- Divide between the prepared cake tins and bake, in batches, for 30–35 minutes, or until a toothpick inserted in the centre comes out clean.

- Cool in the tins for 5 minutes, then run a thin knife blade around the edges of the tins. Invert the cake on to a wire rack to cool completely before frosting.

Make the frosting

- Place the icing sugar and cocoa in a mixing bowl or the bowl of a stand mixer and stir to combine.

- Add the vegan butter, half the milk and the vanilla and beat on a high speed until the frosting is smooth and holds peaks. Gradually add the remaining milk, if needed, to achieve the right consistency.

- Transfer the frosting to a piping bag fitted with a round tip.

Recipe Continues Overleaf

* The cake looks spectacular but can be a bit tricky to slice, which is to be expected. You can use a knife or string to score the top and sides of the cake to indicate where you will be slicing. Leave a small gap along the scored lines when adding the fruit to make this easier.

* You can make a two-layer cake by dividing the batter between two 20cm cake tins and baking for 35–40 minutes.

Assemble the cake

- Add a dot of frosting to a cake board the same size as your cake and place the first cake layer on top.

- Pipe a wide ring of frosting on the outer edge of the first layer and inside the ring middle with the conserve if using. Press down lightly so the cake sticks to the frosting. Position the second cake layer on top and repeat.

- Place the final cake layer on top, bottom side up. Press down lightly.

- Spread a layer of frosting over the entire cake using the angled offset spatula. Use a cake scraper to smooth the frosting (a cake turntable is useful at this stage).

- Chill the cake for 30 minutes, then spread a second layer of frosting over the cake. It doesn't need to be perfect as you will be covering it with berries.

Decorate the cake

- Line a plate with paper towels. Slice the strawberries in half and then cut any large ones into slices. Place cut side down on the paper towels to absorb excess moisture, flipping them over after a while.

- Do the same with half the blueberries, raspberries and blackberries, leaving some of the smaller ones whole.

- Press the sliced strawberries randomly around the cake, spaced apart. Fill any gaps with the blueberries, raspberries, blackberries and frosting.

- Serve immediately once the berries have been added, or store without any fruit for three to four days in an airtight container at room temperature. Serve any berries that are left over on the side, or use in a different recipe, such as the Strawberry & Rhubarb Crumble on page 171 or the Berry Crumble Bars on page 77.

Persian Love Cake

PREP 20 mins
BAKE 45-50 mins
SERVES 10-12

This beautifully fragrant cake is said to have the power to enchant and seduce . . . It certainly has a mesmerizing aroma thanks to the rose water and cardamom. Top with a simple glaze and decorate with chopped pistachios, dried rose petals and Turkish delight.

FOR THE CAKE

200g self-raising flour
60g ground almonds
250g caster sugar
1 tsp baking powder
1 tsp ground cardamom
  (see Notes)
120ml buttermilk
4 medium eggs
115g margarine
½ tsp rosewater
1 tsp vanilla extract

FOR THE GLAZE

180g icing sugar
1 tbsp lemon juice
1 tbsp milk, or as needed
1 tsp rose water, or to taste

TO DECORATE

30g shelled pistachios,
  roughly chopped
1–2 tbsp chopped Turkish
  Delight (optional)
edible rose petals or
  fresh roses

Make the cake

- Mist a deep 20cm cake tin with cake release and line the bottom with baking paper.

- Combine the flour, almonds, sugar, baking powder and cardamom in a mixing bowl.

- Add the buttermilk, eggs, margarine, rose water and vanilla.

- Beat using a hand or stand mixer until the batter is completely smooth, scraping the bottom and sides of the bowl as needed.

- Transfer the batter into the prepared tin and level.

- Preheat the air fryer to 160°C for 3 minutes. Place the cake in the air fryer basket and bake for 45–50 minutes, or until a toothpick inserted in the centre comes out clean.

- Leave in the tin for 5 minutes before inverting on to a wire rack to cool.

NOTES

* Crushing fresh cardamom seeds to a fine powder with a pestle and mortar is far preferable to using ground cardamom, which is much less aromatic.
* Rose water can be overpowering and the strength differs from brand to brand. Add a few drops and increase according to taste.

Recipe Continues Overleaf
● ● ●

Make the glaze and decorate

- Combine all the ingredients for the glaze in a saucepan and stir over a low heat. Add as much milk as needed to create a thick but pourable glaze.

- Spread the glaze over the cooled cake, encouraging it to drip down the sides.

- Decorate with the pistachios, Turkish Delight, if using, and rose petals, then serve.

NOTES

* Turn this into a layer cake using the Victoria sponge buttercream recipe on page 116 to sandwich the layers.

* Slice the cake in half using a cake leveller or a serrated knife. Pipe a layer of frosting over the bottom layer and top with the second. Press down lightly so the cake sticks to the frosting. Spread or pipe any remaining frosting over the top of the cake, leaving the sides visible. Decorate with the pistachios, Turkish Delight, if using, and rose petals.

Whole Orange Cake

PREP 40 mins
BAKE 1 hr 10 mins
SERVES 10-12

This gluten-free orange cake uses whole oranges, peel and all, in the batter. It is incredibly moist and bursting with citrus flavour. Line the cake tin with orange slices to transform the rustic sponge into a spectacular sight when turned upside down. The marmalade glaze adds a glossy mirror-like shine.

TO LINE CAKE TIN

6 tbsp smooth marmalade, warm

3–4 seedless oranges, sliced into thin rounds (250g)

FOR THE CAKE

3 thin-skinned oranges (255g)

250g caster sugar

6 eggs

250g ground almonds

60g fine cornmeal

1 tsp gluten-free baking powder

pinch of salt

TO FINISH

5 tbsp fresh orange juice

4 tbsp smooth marmalade, warm

Prepare the cake tin

- Mist a 20cm springform cake tin with cake release and line the bottom with baking paper.

- Spread the marmalade over the baking paper and position the orange slices over it close together.

Make the batter

- Scrub the oranges clean, pierce with a knife and wrap tightly with foil. Place in the air fryer basket and cook for 30–40 minutes at 185–190°C, turning over halfway (see Notes).

- Check the oranges are soft all the way through when pierced with a knife. If they are still a little hard, add 10 minutes to the cooking time. Leave the oranges to cool slightly, then slice in half and discard any seeds.

- Roughly chop the oranges and blend in a food processor until you have a smooth pulp. Set aside to cool.

- Place the sugar and eggs in a mixing bowl and beat using a hand or stand mixer until frothy.

- Mix in the orange pulp, then add the ground almonds, cornmeal, baking powder and salt until you have a smooth batter.

- Spoon the batter into the orange-lined tin and tap it on the worktop so that the batter settles and air bubbles are released.

- Preheat the air fryer to 170°C for 3 minutes. Place the cake tin in the basket and bake for 60 minutes.

Recipe Continues Overleaf
• • •

- Check the cake is done by inserting a toothpick in the middle – it should come out clean. The internal temperature in the middle of the cake should be over 95°C.

Finishing touches

- Pierce the cake with the toothpick and drizzle the orange juice over it, letting it sink in.

- Cool for 10 minutes, then run a knife blade around the edges of the tin before releasing the cake from the springform tin.

- Carefully invert the cake on to a cake platter or stand and carefully peel the baking paper off – you don't want to dislodge the orange slices.

- Brush the cake with the marmalade to glaze, and serve.

- Store in an airtight container in the fridge for up to five days.

NOTES

* To speed things up, scrub the oranges clean, pierce, then place in a microwave-safe container with a vented lid. Add water to almost cover them and microwave for 10–15 minutes or until the oranges are soft all the way through.

* Use blood oranges if they are in season, as they will make the cake look even more stunning!

6

Delectable
DESSERTS

Baklava

PREP 25 mins
BAKE 45 mins
MAKES 16 squares

Did you know you can bake this irresistibly sweet and sticky baklava with crisp filo pastry and walnut filling in your air fryer? It's a bit of a labour of love and certainly messy, but you will be sweetly rewarded at the end.

FOR THE PASTRY
115g unsalted butter or ghee, melted, plus more as needed
10 sheets filo pastry
1 egg beaten with a little milk, for the egg wash

FOR THE FILLING
300g walnuts
2 tbsp cinnamon

FOR THE SYRUP
350g granulated sugar
200ml water
1 tbsp lemon juice
1 cinnamon stick
small piece of orange peel
few drops of orange flower water (optional)

NOTE Baklava can easily be made vegan – simply use a vegan spread in place of the butter. You will need to weigh down the filo with a wire rack or similar, otherwise the circulating air will cause the top layers of filo to fly off. You can put the melted butter in a spray bottle to make it easy to use.

- Melt the butter. Unwrap the pastry and cut it to fit the shape of your tin. Keep it covered with a slightly damp cloth to prevent it from drying out.

- Pulse the walnuts and cinnamon in a mini chopper or food processor until they are finely ground.

- Brush an 18cm square tin with the melted butter. Stack five sheets of filo on the bottom of the tin, brushing each with melted butter.

- Sprinkle a thin layer of the chopped nuts on top and stack two sheets of filo over them, brushing each sheet with melted butter. Repeat until you have used all the filling. Stack five sheets of pastry on the top.

- Use a sharp knife to score your baklava into squares. Score each square in half on the diagonal. Drizzle any leftover butter over the top.

- Preheat the air fryer to 170°C for 5 minutes. Place the tin in the basket and weigh down with a wire rack. Bake for 40–45 minutes or until golden and crisp.

- Prepare the syrup while the baklava is baking. Combine all the syrup ingredients in a saucepan and stir over a low heat until the sugar is fully dissolved and the syrup has thickened. Discard the cinnamon and orange peel.

- Pour the syrup over the baklava straight out of the air fryer while it is still hot. Allow it to soak through all the layers, then sprinkle with any leftover ground walnuts and leave to cool.

- Use a knife to cut through to the base of the baklava along the scored lines and serve immediately or store for up to two weeks in an airtight container once it has completely cooled.

Pavlova

This sensational pavlova is yet another air fryer triumph! Easy to prepare and totally irresistible, it's filled with softly whipped cream and fresh fruit – the perfect summertime dessert.

PREP 15 mins
BAKE 1 hr 50 mins
SERVES 6

FOR THE PAVLOVA
100ml egg whites from
  a carton
200g caster sugar
¼ tsp cream of tartar
1 tsp lemon juice
1 tsp vanilla bean paste

FOR THE WHIPPED CREAM
240ml double cream, cold
60–80g icing sugar, sifted
1 tsp vanilla bean paste

FOR THE FILLING
2 tbsp lemon or passion fruit
  curd
150g fresh berries or
  4 passion fruit

NOTE If you have leftover meringue, you can make meringue kisses. Place a liner in the air fryer basket. Pipe the meringue kisses spaced slightly apart and bake for 30–40 minutes at 100°C or until dry and easily lifting off the liner. Use them as decorations for the pavlova or any cake. Store in an airtight container.

Make the pavlova

- Place the egg whites, sugar, cream of tartar, lemon juice and vanilla in a bowl over a saucepan of simmering water. Make sure the bottom of the mixing bowl doesn't touch the water.

- Use a balloon whisk to stir the egg whites and sugar to encourage the sugar to dissolve. This will take a few minutes – feel between your fingers; if the mixture feels gritty, then continue to stir.

- Dry the bottom of the mixing bowl and attach to a stand mixer fitted with the whisk attachment. Whisk on maximum speed until the meringue holds glossy, firm peaks.

- Fit a piping bag with a large star tip and fill with the meringue. Place a liner inside your air fryer basket. Pipe a ring of the meringue on the liner then fill the middle. Build up the sides by adding more meringue.

- Bake at 120°C for 20 minutes, then reduce the heat to 95°C and continue to cook for a further 90 minutes. Check whether the pavlova is browning; if so, reduce the temperature by a few degrees.

- Turn the air fryer off but leave the pavlova inside the basket to cool. It can stay in there overnight or until needed.

Make the whipped cream

- Place the whipped cream ingredients in the stand mixer bowl. Beat using the whisk attachment on a medium-low setting until the cream holds soft peaks.

Fill & serve

- Carefully remove the meringue shell from the air fryer and place on a plate. Fill with the whipped cream and lemon curd, and top with a medley of fresh berries or passion fruit pulp. Serve immediately.

Chocolate Basque Cheesecake

PREP 10 mins
BAKE 40 mins
SERVES 8-10
CHILL 5-8 hrs

A chocolate version of the famous 'burnt cheesecake'. This silky crustless cheesecake deserves all the hype and is easy-peasy to make.

200g dark chocolate chips
200g sweetened condensed milk
500g mascarpone cheese
3 eggs
2 tsp vanilla bean paste

- Place the chocolate chips and condensed milk in a microwave-safe bowl and microwave for 30 seconds, then stir and blitz for another 30 seconds. Stir until melted and smooth and set aside to cool.

- Place the mascarpone in a mixing bowl and beat with a hand mixer until creamy and smooth.

- Beat in the eggs and vanilla on a low setting. (You don't want to introduce too much air.)

- Add the melted chocolate mixture and mix it in until the batter is smooth, scraping the bowl with a spatula halfway through.

- Cut two pieces of baking paper large enough to overhang a 20cm springform cake tin. Run them under the tap to wet through and squeeze the water out.

- Line the tin with the paper, clipping on the sides and trimming any excess.

- Pour the batter into the tin and tap gently on the worktop to release air bubbles.

- Place in the air fryer basket and cook for 30 minutes at 160°C. Increase the heat to 180°C and brown the top for 5–10 minutes or until the cheesecake is set around the edges but still a little jiggly in the middle.

- Remove from the air fryer basket and cool for at least an hour. Chill overnight or for at least 5 hours in the fridge before serving.

New York Style Cheesecake

PREP 15 mins
BAKE 45-50 mins
CHILL 8 hrs
SERVES 8-10

Who knew that the air fryer would be so good at baking cheesecakes? No water bath, no fuss and perfect results – I think you'll be converted as soon as you try this recipe!

FOR THE CRUST
180g Biscoff cookies or digestive biscuits
85g unsalted butter, melted

FOR THE FILLING
480g mascarpone
225g full-fat sour cream
400g sweetened condensed milk
2 tsp vanilla bean paste
2 eggs

FOR THE TOPPING
100g granulated sugar
40ml water
2 tbsp lemon juice
1 tsp vanilla extract
½ tbsp cornflour
400g frozen blueberries

Make the crust

- Line the base of an 18cm loose-bottomed cake tin with baking paper. Cover the bottom with a layer of foil, making sure the tin is level. Mist with cake release.

- Pulse the cookies in a mini chopper or food processor until you have fine crumbs. Transfer to a mixing bowl, add the melted butter and stir to combine.

- Add the mix to the lined tin and press down firmly to create an even layer. Chill in the fridge until needed.

Make the filling

- Put the mascarpone, sour cream, condensed milk and vanilla paste in a mixing bowl. Use a hand mixer on a medium speed to beat the ingredients together until well blended.

- Add the eggs and beat on a low speed until the filling is smooth. Use a spatula to scrape the bottom and sides of the bowl as needed.

- Pour the filling over the crust and tap the bottom of the tin gently on the worktop to release any air bubbles. Carefully transfer the tin to the basket of your air fryer.

- Bake at 140°C for 30 minutes. Reduce the temperature to 120°C and bake for 15–20 minutes or until the cheesecake is mostly firm but has a bit of jiggle in the centre. Leave the cheesecake to cool in the air fryer basket after you turn it off.

- Once it has cooled, cover with a plate and chill for 8 hours or overnight.

Recipe Continues Overleaf
● ● ●

Make the topping

- Prepare the topping at the same time as the filling so it can chill in the fridge before using. Place the sugar, water, lemon juice, vanilla and cornflour in a saucepan. Stir to combine.

- Bring to a low simmer and cook until the mix starts to thicken.

- Add the blueberries and stir gently until they start to bubble. Take off the heat and cool at room temperature. Transfer to the fridge to cool completely before using.

Serve

- Run a thin knife blade around the edges of the tin. Carefully release the cheesecake from the tin and transfer to a plate or cake stand.

- Spoon the blueberries over the cheesecake and serve.

NOTES

* The cheesecake will keep for up to two days in the fridge.
* Always use full-fat dairy products in cheesecakes, otherwise they will not set.
* You can use pitted frozen cherries instead of the blueberries in the topping.

Apple Hand Pies

PREP 30 mins
CHILL 30 mins
BAKE 16-20 mins
MAKES 8

These mini Apple Hand Pies are topped with a beautifully crisp pastry lattice. The weaving of the pastry takes a little time but is worth the effort. If you are short on time and patience, feel free to just have a plain pastry top, piercing a few times with a fork to allow the steam to vent.

FOR THE PASTRY

230g plain flour
50g icing sugar
pinch of salt
125g unsalted butter, cold and cubed
2 egg yolks
2 tbsp double cream
1 tsp vanilla extract
icing sugar, for dusting and rolling

FOR THE FILLING

2 apples, peeled and cored (200g chopped weight)
1 tbsp lemon juice
50g soft light brown sugar
20g unsalted butter, cubed
2 tsp cornflour
1 tsp ground cinnamon
¼ tsp ground cloves
¼ tsp ground nutmeg
pinch of salt

FOR THE TOPPING

1 egg yolk, lightly beaten
3 tbsp demerara sugar

TO SERVE (OPTIONAL)

vanilla ice cream

Prepare the pastry

- Sift the flour, icing sugar and salt into a mixing bowl.

- Add the butter and beat on a low speed until the mixture resembles breadcrumbs.

- Combine the egg yolks, double cream and vanilla in a measuring jug. Add to the mixing bowl and very briefly beat together to combine.

- Line your worktop with cling film. Tip the pastry crumbs on to it and use the cling film to gather the pastry together, kneading as needed to form a disc.

- Chill for at least 30 minutes or up to overnight before using.

Prepare the filling

- Chop the apples into pea-sized pieces. Place in a 16cm air fryer cake barrel and toss with the lemon juice, sugar, butter, cornflour, spices and salt.

- Place in the air fryer basket and cook for 10 minutes at 180°C, stirring halfway. Cool before using.

Assemble the pies

- Cut the pastry in half, keeping any you are not using straight away in the fridge covered with cling film.

- Dust your worktop liberally with icing sugar and roll out the pastry to a thickness of 3mm.

- Use a ruler to cut strips that are 1cm wide by 18cm long. Cut in half so they are 9cm long.

Recipe Continues Overleaf
• • •

- Lay six strips horizontally and fold every other strip back on itself. Lay one strip of pie crust vertically over the unfolded strips. Unfold the strips that were pushed back. Now peel back the alternate strips and lay a strip over them.

- Continue swapping the folded and unfolded horizontal strips and adding one new vertical strip each time to create a square lattice. Repeat to create seven more square lattices.

- Roll out the remaining pastry, gathering any scraps and rerolling as needed, and dusting with icing sugar to avoid them sticking.

- Cut eight squares using an 8cm square cutter. Place 2 scant teaspoons of apple filling in the middle of each square and brush the edges with the egg yolk.

- Use a palette knife or spatula to lift each lattice off the worktop. Position over the filling and press the edges down to seal. Use the square cutter to trim the lattice edges.

- Crimp the edges with a fork, brush with egg wash and sprinkle with a little demerara sugar. Repeat until you have eight hand pies.

- Preheat the air fryer to 160°C. Place a wire rack in the basket and mist with sunflower oil. Bake four pies at a time for 16–20 minutes, or until the pies are golden and crisp. Check the underside is cooked – if it looks too pale, continue to cook for a few more minutes.

- Cool before serving or serve warm topped with a small scoop of vanilla ice cream for dessert.

NOTES

* The pastry and filling can be made ahead. Chill for at least 30 minutes before using.

* Reheat the pies in the air fryer for 7–10 minutes before serving.

* The leftover egg whites can be used in the Pavlova on page 151. If you are not using them straight away, lightly beat together and store in a suitable container in the freezer for up to two months, making a note of the weight.

Chocolate Lava Cakes

PREP 15 mins
BAKE 12-14 mins
MAKES 4

The ultimate dessert for chocolate lovers everywhere! These chocolate lava cakes hide a molten centre of pure chocolate indulgence – serve these when you really want to impress.

180g dark chocolate chips

114g unsalted butter, cubed

3 eggs

1 tsp vanilla bean paste

185g icing sugar

60g plain flour

¼ tsp salt

4 tsp cocoa powder

chocolate truffles (white chocolate/salted caramel, etc.)

NOTES

* Lava cakes can be tricky to get right since temperatures vary between air fryer models. Check after 8 minutes and add more time as needed.

* Allow them to cool only slightly before inverting on to a plate – if you leave them for too long, the molten lava centre can set.

* These can be cooked in small ramekins instead of pudding moulds. Serve them as they are in the ramekin – not as impressive to look at but just as delicious and less tricky!

- Put the chocolate chips and butter in a bowl and microwave in 30-second bursts, stirring in between, until completely melted and smooth. Set aside to cool slightly.

- Add the eggs and vanilla and stir to combine using a small balloon whisk. The chocolate will thicken.

- Sift the icing sugar, flour and salt over the chocolate. Fold together until you have a thick glossy batter and no dry streaks remain.

- Spray four 200ml dariole (metal pudding) moulds with cake release or brush with melted butter. Add a scant teaspoon of cocoa powder to each and swirl to cover. Discard any excess cocoa powder.

- Add a large scoop of batter to each of the moulds and top with a chocolate truffle. Cover with some more batter, filling almost to the top of the mould.

- Preheat the air fryer for 3 minutes at 180°C. Place the moulds in the basket, spaced slightly apart. Bake for 10–13 minutes or until the lava cakes have risen in the moulds and the top feels set but not firm (there should still be a bit of a jiggle underneath). You can open the air fryer to check as needed. If you can do a test run I recommend doing one to find out the optimum cooking time for your air fryer.

- Allow to cool for a minute or so, then run a thin knife blade around the edge of the mould to loosen. Carefully invert on to a plate and serve immediately.

Salted Caramel Brownies

PREP 15 mins
BAKE 30-35 mins
MAKES 9 squares

Is there anyone who can resist these dark gooey chocolate brownies with swirls of salted caramel? Not in our house there isn't . . . Serve them warm and topped with vanilla ice cream for dessert or grab a small slice as a treat.

200g dark chocolate chips
115g unsalted butter, cubed
200g light brown sugar
2 tsp vanilla extract
2 eggs
65g plain flour
4 tbsp cocoa powder
pinch of salt
4 tbsp salted caramel
    (optional)

TO SERVE (OPTIONAL)
vanilla ice cream

- Add the chocolate chips and butter to a mixing bowl and microwave for 30-second bursts until the butter melts. Leave to stand for 2 minutes, then stir so that the chocolate melts completely. Set aside.

- Use a balloon whisk to beat the sugar, vanilla and eggs in a separate bowl. Whisk until the sugar is dissolved and the mixture is frothy.

- Stir the melted chocolate mixture into the sugar mixture.

- Sift the flour, cocoa powder and salt into the bowl and stir the mix until you have a smooth thick glossy batter with no pockets of flour.

- Spoon the batter into a greased and lined 20cm square metal cake tin and level. Dollop spoonfuls of salted caramel over the top and use a toothpick to swirl them into the brownie batter.

- Preheat the air fryer to 160°C. Bake the brownies for 30 minutes. The brownies should have a smooth shiny top and feel set at the edges. A toothpick inserted in the middle should come out with a few moist crumbs (but not wet batter). If your brownies are not quite baked, cook for a further 5 minutes.

- Take the tin out of the air fryer and cool the brownies before slicing.

NOTES
* To melt the butter and chocolate in a double boiler, place the bowl over a saucepan of simmering water (not allowing the bowl to be in direct contact with the water) and stir until the chocolate melts.
* Air fryers vary greatly – you might need to adjust the cooking time to suit your model. Add 5 minutes to the cooking time, as needed, and keep checking. Remember that the brownies will become less gooey and more cakey the longer you bake them.
* Store brownies in an airtight container for four to five days. Reheat them for a few seconds in the air fryer for maximum yumminess! Or freeze in portions for up to three months.

Sticky Toffee Puddings

PREP 15 mins
BAKE 20-25 mins
SERVES 6

Sticky toffee pudding is the ultimate dessert to lift spirits on a cold and rainy day. I wish I could bottle their sweet, buttery and spicy aroma, and so will you when these are baking in your air fryer! Serve warm with toffee sauce and some vanilla ice cream.

FOR THE TOFFEE SAUCE
100ml double cream
60g soft light brown sugar
25g soft dark brown sugar
80g unsalted butter, cubed
pinch of salt
1 tbsp dark rum (optional)

FOR THE PUDDINGS
150g pitted soft dates,
    roughly chopped
2-3 globes stem ginger
175ml boiling water
1 tsp bicarbonate of soda
75g unsalted butter,
    softened
150g soft light brown sugar
2 eggs, lightly beaten
175g self-raising flour
2 tsp ground ginger
½ tsp ground cinnamon
generous pinch ground
    cloves
¼ tsp salt

TO SERVE
vanilla ice cream

- Make the toffee sauce by putting all the ingredients apart from the rum in a small saucepan. Stir over a low heat until the butter has melted and the sugar has dissolved.

- Once the sauce is bubbling a little, stir in the rum and cook for 1–2 minutes until it is syrupy. Transfer to a small jug.

- Grease 6 mini pudding moulds with butter and dust them with flour, shaking out any excess.

- Place the dates and stem ginger in the bowl of a mini chopper or food processor fitted with a metal blade. Pour in the boiling water and let it stand for 5 minutes. Pulse until you have a sticky pulp. Stir in the bicarbonate of soda.

- Beat the butter and sugar until fluffy using a stand or hand mixer. Use a spatula to scrape the bottom and sides of the bowl as needed. Add the eggs and a tablespoon of the flour and beat together until incorporated.

- Sift the rest of the flour and all the spices and salt over the bowl and fold them in with a spoon. Stir in the date and ginger pulp.

- Divide the mixture among the moulds, filling about two thirds of the way up. Tap the moulds on your worktop to release any air bubbles, then place in the air fryer basket.

- Bake for 20–25 minutes at 180°C, until the puddings are firm and risen and a skewer inserted in the centre comes out clean.

- Cool them on a wire rack for 5 minutes, then carefully tap them out of the moulds.

- Serve warm with a scoop of vanilla ice cream and plenty of warm toffee sauce for the ultimate indulgence.

Banoffee Poke Cake

PREP 10 mins
BAKE 45-50 mins
SERVES 12

Banoffee pie is my husband's favourite dessert, and I created this cake for his birthday one year. The combination of the soft banana sponge, caramel and whipped cream is simply dreamy!

FOR THE CAKE
200g self-raising flour
150g caster sugar
100g soft light brown sugar
2 small bananas (150g
　peeled weight)
2 eggs
115g unsalted butter,
　softened, or margarine
2 tsp vanilla extract

FOR THE DRIZZLE
250g sweetened condensed
　milk
150g salted caramel (from
　a jar)
2 tbsp double cream

FOR THE FROSTING
300g double cream, cold
80g icing sugar, sifted
1 tbsp custard powder
2 tbsp vanilla bean paste

TO DECORATE
2 tbsp salted caramel
banana chips (optional)

NOTE The cake should be stored in the fridge as the frosting contains fresh cream.

Make the cake

- Mist a 20cm square tin with cake release and line with baking paper.

- Combine the flour and two types of sugar in a mixing bowl, stirring to remove any lumps.

- Mash the bananas using a fork or liquidize in a mini chopper. Add to the flour together the eggs, butter and vanilla. Beat by hand or in a stand mixer until the batter is completely smooth. Use a spatula to scrape the bottom and sides of the bowl as needed.

- Transfer the batter to the prepared cake tin and level.

- Preheat the air fryer to 150°C for 3 minutes. Place the cake tin in the basket and bake for 45–50 minutes. A toothpick inserted in the centre should come out clean.

- Leave the cake to cool in the air fryer basket for 5 minutes. Lift out of the basket and poke holes over the entire cake using a chopstick.

Prepare the drizzle

- Place the condensed milk, caramel and double cream in a saucepan and stir over a low heat until melted.

- Pour a third of the warm drizzle over the cake, letting it in soak in. Repeat until most of the drizzle has been absorbed and leave the cake to cool.

Make the frosting

- Beat all the ingredients on medium speed using a hand or stand mixer until the cream holds peaks. Avoid overbeating as the cream can curdle.

- Transfer the frosting to a piping bag fitted with a large star tip and pipe over the cooled cake. Drizzle with salted caramel and decorate with banana chips, if using, and serve.

Single-Serve Peach Cobbler

PREP 15 mins
BAKE 30 mins
MAKES 4

Warm peach cobbler served with vanilla ice cream feels like the best homey comforting treat. I have used tinned peaches here as fresh peaches tend to be both expensive and a bit insipid in the UK.

FOR THE FRUIT
500g tinned peaches
  (drained weight)
50g soft light brown sugar
50g granulated sugar
1 tsp ground cinnamon
¼ tsp freshly grated nutmeg
1 tsp lemon juice
1 tbsp cornflour

FOR THE TOPPING
130g self-raising flour
50g soft light brown sugar
50g granulated sugar
80g unsalted butter, melted
60ml buttermilk
1 tsp vanilla extract
1 tbsp demerara sugar

TO SERVE
vanilla ice cream or
  single cream

- Cut the peaches into cubes and combine with the rest of the fruit ingredients in a bowl.

- Divide between four large ramekins or similar baking dishes.

- Stir the flour and sugars together in a bowl.

- Combine the melted butter, buttermilk and vanilla and pour into the bowl. Stir briefly with a fork to make a soft crumbly dough.

- Add dollops of the topping to each ramekin, allowing a bit of space for it to expand. Sprinkle with the demerara sugar.

- Preheat the air fryer to 160°C and bake the cobblers, in batches if necessary, for 30 minutes. They are ready when the topping is golden and the fruit filling starts bubbling through.

- Cool for at least 10 minutes and serve warm with vanilla ice cream.

NOTE You can replace the peaches with any fruit you like, such as apples, pears, plums or berries. If you are using stone fruit, you will need to bake it for 10–15 minutes first at 170°C so it can soften before adding the topping.

Strawberry & Rhubarb Crumble

PREP 15 mins
BAKE 30-35 mins
SERVES 4-6

Rainy days call for crumble – it's just the most comforting bake I can think of and one of the easiest to throw together. I have used rhubarb and strawberries here, but you can use whatever fruit is in season. It's delicious on its own or paired with custard or ice cream for dessert.

VEGAN/GLUTEN-FREE

FOR THE FILLING

400g strawberries, sliced in half

400g fresh rhubarb, cut into small pieces

30g vegan butter, cubed

6 tbsp light brown sugar

2 tsp cornflour

1 tbsp lemon juice

2 tsp vanilla extract

FOR THE CRUMBLE

200g rolled oats

50g rice flour or gluten-free flour

50g demerara sugar

¼ tsp baking powder

60g vegan butter, cubed

1 tsp ground cinnamon

¼ tsp salt

SERVING SUGGESTIONS

custard

vanilla ice cream

Prepare & cook the filling

- Preheat the air fryer to 180°C.

- Put all the filling ingredients into a 16cm baking dish. Stir to combine. Cook for 20 minutes, or until the fruit has started to soften.

Make the crumble topping

- Put the oats, rice flour, sugar, baking powder, vegan butter, cinnamon and salt in bowl. Toss together, rubbing the butter into the dry ingredients with your fingers until small clumps form.

- Add the oat crumble over the cooked fruit. Reduce the temperature to 160°C and bake for a further 15 minutes, or until the topping is golden and the fruit filling starts to bubble through the sides.

- Rest the crumble for 10–15 minutes so that the filling cools and thickens.

- Serve warm topped with vanilla ice cream or custard.

NOTE Some pairings for you to try:
* Apple and blackberries
* Plum and apples
* Pear and ginger

7

Savoury
BAKES

Spicy Feta Rolls

PREP 20 mins
AIR FRY 10 mins
MAKES 8

My husband's favourite Greek dip is *tyrokafteri*, which translates as 'spicy cheese'. Here I have used it as the filling for these crisp vegetarian filo feta rolls – they are addictive!

FOR THE FILLING
400g feta cheese
200g roasted peppers (from a jar)
1 tsp sriracha (optional)
2 tsp fresh thyme leaves

FOR THE PASTRY
12 filo pastry sheets, or as needed
200g unsalted butter or ghee, melted, as needed

FOR THE SPICY HONEY
115g honey
2 tsp chilli flakes
2 tsp fresh thyme leaves

NOTES
* You can store the rolls, once they have cooled, in an airtight container for up to three days in the fridge.
* Refresh the pastry and warm them up in an air fryer at 180°C for 3–5 minutes.
* Store leftover spicy honey in a jar and use within a week.

- Add the filling ingredients to a mini chopper or food processor and pulse a few times to make a coarse paste.

- Cut a pack of filo pastry in half so that you have two stacks of pastry squares. Keep the filo covered with a slightly damp cloth while you are working so it doesn't dry out.

- Lay one filo square on your worktop and brush with the ghee. Layer two more sheets of filo over the top, brushing each with ghee.

- Spoon three small scoops of filling about 5cm in from the border on the pastry closest to you. Don't overfill! Brush with ghee and fold the edges in to encase the filling.

- Fold the edge closest to you over the filling and then roll, burrito-style, to make a neat parcel. Remember to always brush each sheet of pastry with ghee so that the pastry sticks together and crisps up when baked.

- Repeat with the remaining pastry and filling. Keep the rolls covered with a damp cloth until you are ready to cook.

- Preheat the air fryer to 200°C for 3 minutes. Place three rolls on a rack or directly in the air fryer basket and cook for 5 minutes at 180°C.

- Gently flip the rolls over and cook for 5 minutes or until crisp and golden. Transfer to a wire rack to cool slightly while you air fry the rest of the rolls.

- To make the spicy honey, add the honey, chilli flakes and thyme to a saucepan and heat gently for a few minutes, stirring to combine. You want the chilli to infuse the honey with a hint of spice. Keep warm until ready to serve.

- Drizzle the warm rolls with the spicy honey and serve immediately as a shared meze or with a salad for lunch.

Spanakopita Triangles

PREP 20 mins
AIR FRY 14 mins
MAKES 9

These delicious Greek Spanakopita Triangles are fabulous as a party appetizer or on-the-go snack. The crisp filo pastry is filled with spinach, feta cheese and lots of herbs.

250g baby spinach

2 tsp sea salt flakes

20g fresh dill, finely chopped

2 tbsp fresh mint, finely chopped

200g vegetarian feta cheese, crumbled

150g garlic and herb cream cheese

1 egg

1 tsp garlic powder

9 sheets filo pastry

60–80g unsalted butter or ghee, melted

- Finely chop the spinach and sprinkle with the salt, tossing to combine. Leave for 10 minutes, then place the spinach in a clean tea towel and wring out the moisture. Place in a mixing bowl and add the herbs, feta, cream cheese, egg and garlic powder and mix well.

- Open the pack of filo pastry and keep any you are not using straight away covered with a damp cloth.

- Lay one sheet of filo on your worktop and brush with melted butter. Fold the filo in half lengthwise.

- Place two tablespoons of filling on the corner edge of pastry closest to you.

- Fold the end of your strip with the filling over to form a triangle. Continue folding the pastry, brushing sparingly with butter, until you have a neatly folded triangle. Brush with butter on both sides.

- Repeat until you have used up all the filling – you should have enough for nine triangles.

- Preheat the air fryer for 3 minutes at 180°C. Spray a wire rack with olive oil and place in air fryer basket. Cook the triangles in batches for 12–14 minutes, flipping over halfway through. Cool slightly before serving.

NOTE The triangles can be kept for two to three days in a covered container in the fridge. Reheat in the air fryer for 5–10 minutes at 180°C to crisp up the pastry.

Ultimate Sausage Rolls

PREP 10 mins
AIR FRY 14 mins
MAKES 18

These sausage rolls are dangerously tasty and tend to mysteriously disappear before they have even cooled down properly. These are sure to go down a storm at parties – the combination of flaky pastry, chorizo and sausage is impossible to resist.

FOR THE SAUSAGE ROLLS
320g puff pastry
100g cooking chorizo
(sweet or spicy)
350g sausage meat
(or from 6 sausages)
4 slices prosciutto

FOR THE EGG WASH
1 egg, lightly beaten

FOR THE TOPPINGS
3 tbsp sesame seeds
3 tbsp nigella seeds

- Take the puff pastry out of the fridge and let it come to room temperature for 10 minutes.

- Remove the casings from the chorizo and blitz in a mini chopper until you have a coarse paste.

- Place in a mixing bowl, together with the sausage meat, and mix using your hands or a wooden spoon until well combined.

- Unroll the pastry, keeping it on the paper it came wrapped in. Slice it in half lengthwise.

- Place the prosciutto slices over the pastry, leaving a small border at one end.

- Shape the sausage meat into a thin log the length of your pastry. Position on one side of the pastry over the prosciutto.

- Brush the border with the egg wash and roll the pastry to encase the filling, pressing down to seal.

- Slice into nine equal pieces using a serrated knife. Repeat with the remaining filling and pastry.

- Brush the rolls with egg wash and sprinkle half the rolls with the sesame seeds and half with the nigella seeds.

- Preheat the air fryer to 200°C. Spray the basket with sunflower oil and place the rolls in the basket, spaced slightly apart. You will need to cook in two or three batches to avoid overcrowding.

- Cook for 7 minutes, then flip over and cook for a further 7 minutes or until the pastry is puffed and golden. Cool slightly before serving.

Spring Rolls

PREP 15 mins
AIR FRY 16 mins
MAKES 14-16

Easiest-ever spring rolls in your air fryer! Using stir-fry mix and ready-cooked rice noodles cuts down on prep so you can enjoy these all the quicker. Serve with sweet chilli sauce on the side as a shared starter.

1 tbsp toasted sesame seed oil, or as needed
600g stir-fry mix
300g pork mince, 20% fat
4 tbsp oyster sauce
2 tbsp sambal oelek chilli paste
2 tbsp soy sauce
1 tbsp cornflour
300g straight-to-wok thin rice noodles
16 sheets filo pastry
sweet chilli sauce, to serve

NOTES

* The stir-fry vegetable mix should contain a mix of peppers, cabbage, carrots and bamboo shoots.
* Make a vegan version by replacing the pork with a suitable plant-based alternative and using vegetarian oyster sauce.
* Store in the fridge for up to three days, reheating in the air fryer for 7–10 minutes at 180°C before serving.
* Replace the sambal oelek with a tablespoon of sriracha if needed.

- Heat the sesame oil in a wok and stir-fry the vegetables for 2 minutes until slightly softened but still crunchy. Transfer to a bowl to cool.

- Add a little more oil if needed and stir-fry the mince until browned, about 3–4 minutes. Drain any fat that has rendered and add the mince to the vegetables.

- Combine the oyster sauce, chilli paste, soy sauce and cornflour in a small bowl.

- Use scissors to snip the rice noodles or roughly chop them with a knife. Add to the vegetables and mince, together with the sauce mix, and toss to combine.

- Unroll the filo pastry and keep it covered with a damp cloth to prevent it from drying out. Lay one sheet on your worktop and brush with sesame oil. Fold in half to form a square.

- Position the pastry so that one corner is facing you. Place two tablespoons of filling a couple of centimetres in from the corner closest to you. Brush the pastry with oil.

- Fold the corner closest to you over the filling and then fold in the corners either side of it to encase the filling.

- Fold the little parcel into a roll, brushing the pastry as needed with oil. Repeat until you have used all the filling and pastry.

- Preheat the air fryer to 180°C for 3 minutes. Add 3–4 rolls, spaced slightly apart.

- Cook for 7 minutes, then turn and cook for a further 7 minutes, or until the rolls are crisp and golden. Cool on a wire rack while you cook the rest of the rolls.

- Serve warm with sweet chilli sauce.

Cornbread Muffins with Honey Butter

PREP 5 mins
BAKE 18 mins
MAKES 6

There's nothing complex about cornbread muffins, but I could literally eat them every day. Split them in half as soon as they're cool enough to handle, spread with the spicy honey butter and prepare to swoon!

350ml buttermilk

85g butter, melted

2 eggs

50g honey

2 tsp hot sauce, such as sriracha (optional)

200g plain flour

100g fine cornmeal

½ tbsp baking powder

½ tsp bicarbonate of soda

½ tsp salt

FOR THE HONEY BUTTER

4 tbsp unsalted butter, softened

2 tbsp honey

large pinch sea salt flakes

1 tsp hot sauce, or more to taste

- Combine the buttermilk, butter, eggs, honey and hot sauce in a mixing bowl. Stir well to combine.

- Sift the flour, cornmeal, baking powder, bicarbonate of soda and salt into the bowl.

- Gently fold the dry ingredients into the wet until no dry streaks remain.

- Mist a six-hole muffin tin (or six pudding moulds) with cake release or grease them with butter. Place in the air fryer basket.

- Divide the batter evenly between the muffin tin holes and bake for 15 minutes at 180°C.

- Flip the muffins directly into the air fryer basket and bake for 3–5 minutes to brown the bottoms.

- Combine the softened butter, honey, salt and hot sauce in a small bowl and serve with the warm muffins.

NOTE If you have leftovers, you can make cornbread croutons. Slice the muffins into small cubes and toss with a little olive oil. Bake for 10–15 minutes at 160°C in the air fryer, shaking the basket once or twice. Use them in salads or soups.

Pull-Apart Garlic Bread

PREP 15 mins
AIR FRY 20 mins
SERVES 6-8

Use one of your air fryer loaves to create this insanely tasty garlic bread! It is garlicky, cheesy and impossible to resist – perfect for sharing during a party or as a starter at dinner. You can even prepare it ahead of time and air fry it just before serving.

6 large garlic cloves, unpeeled

1 tbsp olive oil

100g unsalted butter, softened

1 tbsp fresh parsley or chives (optional)

pinch of sea salt

1 small round bread loaf (such as No-Knead Bread or Beginner's Overnight Sourdough, see pages 198 & 216)

100g firm, low-moisture mozzarella, grated or shredded

olive oil, to drizzle, as needed

- Place the garlic cloves on a small piece of foil and drizzle with the olive oil. Wrap them in the foil to cover them. Air fry for 5 minutes at 190°C or until the garlic has softened.

- Squeeze the garlic out of the skin into a mini chopper. Add the butter, parsley and salt, and blitz to a spreadable paste. You can add a little boiling water if you need to loosen the garlic butter.

- Place two wooden spoons on either side of your bread, then use a bread knife to slice the bread in one direction. (The wooden spoon will stop you from cutting all the way through the bread.)

- Turn the bread clockwise and slice in the other direction, again using the spoons to prevent from cutting through the bread completely.

- Place the loaf on a large piece of baking paper. Use a knife or your fingertips to prise apart the bread and smear the garlic butter all over, going as far down as you can. This is quite a messy job!

- Do the same with the shredded mozzarella, then drizzle the whole loaf with a little olive oil. Wrap the bread in the baking paper and then a layer of foil.

- Air fry for 15 minutes at 180°C, then open the parcel and cook for a further 5 minutes or until the cheese has melted.

- Cool for 5 minutes before serving.

NOTE Roasting the garlic first mellows the flavour considerably. You can also add some fresh minced garlic if you are after a stronger garlic taste.

Pinsa Pizza

Pinsa – also known as Roman pizza – dates back to ancient Rome. The dough has a unique crispy crust but is fluffy and airy inside thanks to the combination of pasta, rice and spelt flours. This recipe makes enough dough for four air fryer pizza bases, each serving one, that you can customize with your favourite toppings.

PREP 20 mins
FERMENTATION 2–3 days
BAKE 12–16 mins
MAKES 4 pizza bases

VEGAN (BASE)

FOR THE DOUGH
380g pasta flour
2 tbsp rice flour, plus extra for rolling
2 tbsp spelt or soy flour
1 tbsp sugar
1½ tsp salt
½ tsp rapid-rise yeast
300ml water
1 tbsp olive oil, or as needed

TOPPING SUGGESTIONS
pizza sauce or pesto
mozzarella cheese, block or shredded
pepperoni, prosciutto, chorizo or similar
roasted vegetables
fresh basil

Prepare the dough

- Combine the flours, sugar, salt and yeast in a mixing bowl. Add the water and olive oil and stir with a wooden spoon or dough hook until you have a shaggy dough. Cover with greased cling film and rest for 30 minutes.

- Mix again using oiled hands until the dough is a bit smoother – it's not necessary to knead. Place in an oiled covered container with plenty of space for the dough to expand, and refrigerate for two to three days.

Make the pizza base

- Dust your worktop with rice flour and scoop the dough on to it. Divide into four equal pieces and roll each into a ball. Cover with greased cling film and rest for 30 minutes.

- Dust a baking liner or silicone mat with rice flour. Flatten one of the balls of dough on to it, gently stretching with your fingers to form a disc. Use your fingertips to flatten the middle and create slightly raised edges. Drizzle with a little olive oil.

- Preheat the air fryer to 200°C for 5 minutes. Place the pizza in the basket and cook for 6–8 minutes, flipping over halfway through. Repeat with the rest of the dough if you are using all of it.

Add toppings & bake

- Spread pizza sauce over the base and add cheese plus your favourite toppings.

- Bake for 6–8 minutes at 170–180°C or until the cheese is bubbling and the crust is crisp. Slice and enjoy!

Yorkshire Puddings

PREP 5 mins
REST 30 mins
AIR FRY 15 mins
MAKES 12 small
puddings

No Sunday roast is complete without Yorkshire puddings and the good news is you can easily make them in your air fryer.

130g plain flour
½ tsp salt
3 eggs
240ml milk, semi-skimmed

TO COOK
3 tbsp vegetable cooking fat
   or goose fat, or as needed

Make the batter

- Measure the flour into a mixing bowl. Add the salt and stir to combine. Crack the eggs into the bowl, add a splash of the milk and use a balloon whisk to whisk together.

- Gradually add the remaining milk and mix until you have a smooth batter. Rest the batter for 30 minutes or overnight in the refrigerator (covered).

Preheat the air fryer

- Place a six-hole silicone muffin tin (or use pudding tins) in the air fryer basket. Add half a teaspoon of vegetable cooking fat (or goose fat) to each. Preheat the air fryer at 200°C for 5 minutes.

- Stir the batter well before making the puddings. If it still feels a bit lumpy, you can sieve it before using.

- Working quickly, pour the batter into the holes/tins to just under halfway up. Air fry for 10 minutes – the puddings will look golden and puffed up on top but still a bit doughy underneath.

- Use tongs to flip them over directly into the air fryer basket and cook for another 5 minutes or until golden, puffed, with crisp edges and as light as air. If they still feel heavy, you can continue cooking them for a little longer.

- Cook in batches until you have used up all the batter. You can refresh the yorkies just before serving by reheating them for 5 minutes in the air fryer at 180°C.

NOTE If you have an immersion blender, you can add all the ingredients into a tall measuring jug and blitz until the batter is smooth.

Beef Empanadas

PREP 20 mins
CHILL 1+ hr
AIR FRY 12-14 mins
MAKES 8-10

There's a shop near me that sells the most amazing empanadas. After trying them, I knew I had to try to recreate them at home – in the air fryer, of course. They were a huge hit with the family and have become a firm favourite.

FOR THE DOUGH

200g plain flour, plus extra
  for dusting and rolling
1 tbsp granulated sugar
½ tsp baking powder
½ tsp salt
60ml ice-cold water
1 tbsp white wine vinegar
113g cold unsalted butter,
  cubed

FOR THE FILLING

1 large onion, peeled and
  roughly chopped
3 garlic cloves, peeled
1 beef stock cube, crumbled,
  or 2 tsp beef bouillon
  powder
1 tbsp soft light brown sugar
1 tbsp cumin
1 tsp sweet smoked paprika
½ tsp cayenne
1 tsp garlic granules
½ tsp salt
2 tbsp olive oil
450g minced beef, 15% fat
½ tbsp dried oregano
1 tbsp tomato paste
45ml red wine
50g pitted green olives,
  finely chopped (optional)
1 hard-boiled egg, finely
  chopped (optional)

Make the dough

- Put the flour, sugar, baking powder and salt in the bowl of a food processor fitted with a metal blade. Pulse to combine.

- Combine the water and vinegar in a glass.

- Add the cubed butter to the food processor and pulse a few times, until the butter is blended into the flour in smallish pieces (about the size of a pea).

- Drip feed the water through the processor tube and pulse until the dough starts forming clumps. If you pinch a piece between your fingertips, it should hold together.

NOTE add only as much water as needed for the dough to reach this stage; you may not need to use it all.

- Cover your worktop with cling film and tip the dough on to it. Gather the dough into a ball, using the cling film to push it together. Flatten to a disc and wrap with cling film. Chill for at least an hour or overnight before using.

NOTE you can add flour, as needed, if the dough is very sticky.

Prepare the filling

- Place the onion, garlic, stock cube, sugar, spices, garlic granules and salt in a mini chopper and pulse until minced. You can also dice the onion by hand or use a box grater.

- Heat the olive oil in a large frying pan. Add the onion mixture and stir over a medium heat for 5–10 minutes, or until the onion has softened.

- Stir in the beef, breaking it up with the back of your wooden spoon.

Recipe Continues Overleaf

SERVING SUGGESTIONS (OPTIONAL)
tomato salsa
tomatillo salsa

- Once the beef has browned a little, add the oregano, tomato paste and wine and continue to cook, stirring, until the beef is cooked through.

- Stir in the chopped olives and hard-boiled egg, if using.

- Transfer the filling to a bowl and allow it to cool before using. You can also prepare it a day ahead together with the dough and keep it chilled until needed.

Prepare the empanadas

- Lightly dust your worktop and rolling pin with flour. Put the egg yolk in a small bowl and beat it lightly with a fork.

- Cut the dough into two pieces, keeping any you aren't using covered with cling film. Roll out the dough to a thickness of 3mm and cut out 10cm circles using a bowl to guide you.

- Place about a tablespoon of filling on each round of dough and spread it out slightly, leaving a small border. Don't overfill.

- Brush the border with the egg yolk and fold the dough to enclose the filling.

- Crimp the edge with your fingertips or use a fork to seal the empanadas. Continue until you have used all the dough and filling.

- Brush the empanadas with the egg yolk on the top (but not the underside).

- Preheat the air fryer to 200°C. Mist the air fryer basket liberally with sunflower oil.

- Place the empanadas in the air fryer basket and cook, in batches, for 12–14 minutes, flipping halfway through.

- Transfer to a wire rack to cool slightly before serving as a snack with salsa or as a main meal with a salad on the side.

NOTES
* Use the leftover egg whites for the Pavlova on page 151.
* You can easily make a vegetarian version by replacing the minced beef with a vegetarian alternative.
* For a vegan version, use vegan butter in the dough. Prepare the filling using vegan mince, leaving out the egg, omitting the egg wash and instead misting the empanadas with oil.

Vegan Wellington

This vegan 'wellington' contains a medley of mushrooms, spinach, chestnuts and barley to create a hearty dish that's great for sharing at a dinner party. Serve warm with lashings of onion gravy. YUM!

PREP 20 mins
BAKE 35-40 mins
MAKES 2 wellingtons, each serving 4

VEGAN

FOR THE FILLING

100g baby spinach

½ tsp sea salt flakes

400g chestnut mushrooms

1 tbsp olive oil

1 tsp salt

1 tsp garlic granules

2 tsp herbes de Provence

250g cooked barley or brown lentils (from a pouch)

180g cooked chestnuts, roughly chopped

50g dried cranberries, roughly chopped

50g pine nuts

1 tbsp white miso paste (optional)

1 tbsp panko breadcrumbs

2 tbsp fresh sage, finely chopped

FOR THE PASTRY

2 packs vegan puff pastry

3 tbsp oat milk, to brush

Prepare the filling

- Chop the spinach, place in a bowl and sprinkle with the sea salt flakes. Leave to stand for 5 minutes while you cook the mushrooms.

- Roughly chop the mushrooms and place in the air fryer basket. dd the olive oil, salt, garlic granules and herbs and give the basket a good shake to combine the ingredients.

- Cook for 5 minutes at 190°C, shaking the basket once, until the mushrooms are browned. Transfer them to a mixing bowl, along with any juices that have been released while cooking.

- Place the spinach in a clean tea towel and wring out most of the moisture. Add to the mixing bowl.

- Stir in all the remaining filling ingredients and leave to cool.

Assemble & bake

- Take the puff pastry out of the fridge and allow it to come to room temperature for 10 minutes.

- Unroll one of the pastry packages, keeping it on the paper it comes in. Place in front of you with the long side facing you.

- Place approximately half the filling on the right-hand side of the rectangle of pastry, leaving a 2cm border. Brush the border with the oat milk.

- Fold the left edge of the pastry over to encase the filling and press the edges to seal. Crimp with a fork and trim any excess. You can use the trimmings to create some decorative shapes to add to the top of the wellington if you like.

- Brush the wellington with oat milk and poke a few holes in the top to allow steam to escape.

SAVOURY BAKES
193

Recipe Continues Overleaf
• • •

FOR THE VEGAN ONION GRAVY

1 tbsp vegan butter

1 white onion, sliced thinly

½ tsp salt

pinch of brown sugar

1 tbsp plain flour

1 tsp Dijon mustard

480ml vegetable stock
   (made with 2 stock cubes),
   hot

2 tbsp soy sauce

salt and pepper, to taste

- Repeat this with the second pack of pastry and filling. You can bake this now or freeze it to serve another time (see Notes).

- Preheat the air fryer to 185–190°C for 5 minutes. Transfer the wellington, using the paper, to the basket and bake for 35–40 minutes or until the pastry is puffed and golden

Make the gravy

- Prepare the gravy while you bake the wellington. Melt the vegan butter in a frying pan over a medium-low heat.

- Add the onion, salt and sugar and fry for 10 minutes, stirring often, until it's softened but not browned.

- Stir in the flour and mustard and cook for 1 minute.

- Gradually add the vegetable stock, stirring all the while, then add the soy sauce and simmer until the gravy thickens. Taste and adjust the seasoning if needed.

- Strain the gravy and discard the onions.

Serve & enjoy

- Allow the pastry to cool slightly before slicing with a serrated knife and serving with the gravy.

NOTES

* Freeze for up to six weeks and air fry from frozen, adding 10–15 minutes to the cooking time.

* You can prepare the recipe a day ahead and reheat in the air fryer for 10–15 minutes at 180°C before serving.

8

Bread &
YEASTED
DOUGH

No-Knead Bread

PREP 10 mins
PROVE 1-1½ hrs
BAKE 45 mins
MAKES 1 small loaf

If bread-baking scares you, then this easy no-knead bread will ease you into the wonderful world of yeasted bakes. Nothing beats fresh home-made bread and the pride you will feel when slicing through the crust is priceless.

285g strong white bread
  flour, plus extra for dusting
1 tsp rapid-rise yeast
1 tsp salt
1 tsp sugar
250ml water or beer (I used
  non-alcoholic lager)
fine semolina for the tin

- Add the flour, yeast, salt and sugar to a mixing bowl and stir to combine.

- Stir in the water or beer with a wooden spoon to make a wet and sticky dough.

- Mist the bowl with oil spray and cover with greased cling film. Leave the dough to rise for 1–1½ hours, or until doubled.

- Grease a deep 17cm air fryer cake barrel with oil and sprinkle with the semolina, turning so it coats the bottom and sides.

- Tip the bread dough on to a well-floured worktop. Use a silicone scraper or spatula to fold the edges over towards the middle to create a round loaf (it will be quite sticky and loose).

- Transfer to the cake barrel, cover with greased cling film and leave to rise for 30 minutes.

- Preheat the air fryer to 200°C for 5 minutes. Add the cake barrel to the air fryer basket and add a couple of ice cubes into the basket to create steam.

- Bake for 25 minutes, then reduce the temperature to 180°. Take the cake barrel out using oven mitts and loosen the bread from the edges if needed. Invert on to a wire rack.

- Place the bread back into the air fryer basket, bottom side up. Continue to bake for a further 15–20 minutes or until the bread sounds hollow when you tap the underside. The internal temperature should be 98°C.

- Cool on a wire rack before slicing.

NOTE Wrap the bread in a clean linen towel and store at room temperature for up to three days. Alternatively, slice and freeze for up to two months, toasting a slice from frozen to serve.

Kinda Bagels

OK, these are not *really* bagels – for one thing, there's no yeast.
They use just a handful of ingredients and are super easy to make.

240g Greek-style yogurt
240g self-raising flour
1 tsp garlic and herb
   seasoning
½ tsp salt
¼ tsp sugar
a little olive oil
1 egg beaten with
   1 tsp cream, to brush
2 tbsp sesame seeds

- Combine the yogurt, flour, seasoning, salt and sugar in a mixing bowl using a spoon or a hand mixer fitted with dough hooks.

- Cover the bowl with a damp tea towel and rest for 10 minutes.

- Drizzle a little olive oil over your hands and briefly knead until the dough comes together.

- Roll the dough out on to a lightly floured worktop to a thickness of 2½cm. Use a doughnut cutter to cut out eight bagels, gathering the dough scraps and rerolling as needed. Mist the bagels with sunflower oil.

- Place the bagels on a paper liner over a wire rack (you will need to bake in batches). Bake in a preheated air fryer at 180°C for 7 minutes then flip over.

- Brush the top with the egg wash and sprinkle with sesame seeds. Bake for a further 7 minutes or until golden. Cool before slicing.

NOTE You can use these bagels instead of brioche to make the Baked Eggs and Ham on page 41.

Brioche

Brioche is made with an enriched dough that contains milk, butter and eggs. It tastes delicious on its own and can also be used to make French toast, bread-and-butter pudding, croque-monsieur and other sweet and savoury treats.

PREP 20 mins
PROVE + CHILL 4+ hrs
BAKE 35–40 mins
MAKES 1 loaf

FOR THE BRIOCHE
60ml semi-skimmed milk
113g unsalted butter, cubed
3 eggs
260g bread flour, plus extra
   for dusting and rolling
3 tbsp caster sugar
7g rapid-rise yeast
¾ tsp salt

FOR THE EGG WASH
1 egg beaten with ½ tbsp
   milk

Prepare the dough

- Place the milk in a saucepan and heat until bubbles appear around the edge. Take the pan off the heat and stir in the butter until it melts. Leave to cool.

- Add the eggs and stir to combine.

- Combine the flour, sugar, yeast and salt in the bowl of a stand mixer fitted with a dough hook.

- Add the contents of the saucepan and beat on medium-low for 10 minutes. The dough will be very sticky.

First rise

- Mist a large glass or plastic container with sunflower oil and add the dough. Leave the dough to rise until almost doubled – this can take 2–3 hours or longer.

- Place the dough in the fridge for 1 hour to firm up.

Second rise

- Mist a deep 900g loaf tin with cake release.

- Lightly dust your worktop with flour and tip the dough on to it, pressing lightly to deflate.

- Divide into three equal pieces (190g) and roll each into a 33cm-long rope. Pinch the edges to seal and braid. Tuck the ends of the braid underneath and place in the prepared tin.

- Cover loosely with greased cling film and leave to rise for 2 hours.

Recipe Continues Overleaf

• • •

Bake

- Brush the loaf with the egg wash.

- Remove the rack from the air fryer if your model has one. Preheat the air fryer to 180°C for 3 minutes. Add the loaf tin to the basket and lower the temperature to 150°C. Bake for 35–40 minutes or until the internal temperature is 87°C.

- Cool on a wire rack before slicing and serving.

- Store the cooled bread in a paper bag inside an airtight container or bread bin for up to five days. Alternatively, you can freeze the sliced loaf and toast a slice from frozen whenever you get a craving!

NOTES

* To check whether the brioche dough is ready to use, press it lightly with a finger. The dough should spring back slowly, leaving an indentation.

* Although this recipe takes a long time to complete, most of it is hands-off. You can prepare the dough and refrigerate for 16 hours or for up to two days before baking. This allows the flavour of the brioche to intensify and makes the dough easier to shape.

* Use any leftover brioche to make the Churro French Toast Sticks on page 21 or the Brioche-Baked Eggs and Ham on page 41.

Potato Tear-&-Share Bread

PREP 30 mins
PROVE 2+ hrs
BAKE 20-25 mins
MAKES 10 small rolls

This delicious tear & share bread uses potatoes to create a beautifully soft crumb. It's ideal for serving as a starter with dips or as a companion to charcuterie and cheese boards.

FOR THE BREAD

125g Maris Piper potatoes, peeled and cubed

120ml potato cooking water, cooled

30g unsalted butter

230g strong white bread flour, plus extra for dusting

1½ tsp rapid-rise yeast

1 tbsp sugar

1 tsp salt

1 tsp garlic granules

1 tsp fresh rosemary, very finely chopped

1 tbsp olive oil, for the bowl

TOPPINGS

4 tbsp butter, melted

3 tbsp sesame seeds

3 tbsp nigella seeds

generous pinch salt flakes

Prepare the dough

- Boil the potatoes until fork-tender. Drain and reserve 120ml of the cooking water. Leave to cool.

- Mash the potatoes and butter until smooth. Set aside to cool.

- Put the flour, yeast, sugar, salt and garlic granules in a mixing bowl or the bowl of your stand mixer. Stir to combine.

- Add the mashed potatoes, rosemary and half the cooled water and beat on a low speed until the ingredients start coming together.

- Keep adding the water until the dough forms a ball and starts to pull away from the edges of the bowl. If the dough is too sticky, add an additional tablespoon of flour.

- Grease the bowl with the oil, cover and leave the dough to rise for 60–90 minutes or until doubled.

Shape & rise

- Line a 20cm round cake tin with baking paper and brush with melted butter. Place a small ramekin in the middle of the tin and brush the sides and top with butter.

- Put the sesame seeds, nigella seeds and remaining melted butter in three separate shallow bowls.

- Turn the dough out on to a lightly floured surface and knock it back. Let it rest for 5 minutes, then form it into a long sausage shape.

- Divide the dough into ten pieces. Roll each into a small ball.

Recipe Continues Overleaf
• • •

- Brush the rolls with the melted butter and dip three into the sesame seeds, three into the nigella seeds and leave four plain.

- Arrange in the prepared cake tin, alternating the toppings, and sprinkle with the salt. Leave to rise for 40 minutes.

- Preheat the air fryer to 180°C for 3 minutes. Add the cake tin to the air fryer basket and bake for 20–25 minutes, or until the bread is golden and the internal temperature is above 95°C, covering with foil after 15 minutes. Invert the bread on to a wire rack and remove the ramekin. Flip over on to a plate and serve.

NOTE You can present the bread with a bowl of extra-virgin olive oil and balsamic vinegar for dipping, or serve as a shared starter with a cheese or charcuterie board.

Tiger Rolls

Tiger rolls are so called because of the mottled pattern on their crust. They have a soft crumb and an irresistibly crunchy crust – bake them once and you will be hooked!

PREP 15 mins
PROVE 2+ hrs
BAKE 25 mins
MAKES 6

FOR THE BREAD

210ml warm water or beer (lager)
40g unsalted butter, softened
2½ tbsp granulated sugar
2 tsp salt
360g strong white bread flour
1 tsp rapid-rise yeast

FOR THE TOPPING

4 level tbsp rice flour
¼ tsp rapid-rise yeast
1 tbsp granulated sugar
1 tsp yeast extract
3 tbsp water
½ tbsp sesame oil

- Combine the water or beer, butter, sugar and salt in a measuring jug and leave it until the butter melts. Allow this to cool to just barely warm before using.

- Place the flour and yeast in a mixing bowl and stir to combine. Pour in the liquid ingredients and stir to combine. Knead by hand or using a hand or stand mixer until the dough becomes smooth and elastic.

- Mist the bowl with oil spray and cover with greased cling film. Leave to rise for 60–90 minutes, or until doubled.

- Punch the dough down to deflate. Divide into six equal pieces (approx. 105g each). Flatten each to form a disc, then pinch the edges inwards to make a roll. Repeat with the rest of the dough to make six rolls.

- Place on a greased liner, spaced slightly apart. Leave the rolls to rise for 10 minutes.

Make the topping

- Combine all the ingredients in the order listed and make a spreadable paste. If the paste is too watery, stir in a little more rice flour.

- Brush the top of the rolls with the paste and allow them to rise for a further 20 minutes.

- Preheat the air fryer to 200°C for 5 minutes. Add the rolls and bake for 10 minutes.

- Lower the heat to 190°C and bake for 20 minutes.

- Remove the rolls from the air fryer and flip them over so they are bottom side up.

- Bake for another 5 minutes or until the underside sounds hollow when tapped. Transfer to a wire rack to cool before slicing.

Orange & Cardamom Challah Bread

PREP 20 mins
PROVE 2½ hrs
BAKE 35–40mins
MAKES 1 small loaf

This beautifully fragrant bread is enriched with eggs and oil and tastes sensational toasted and spread with honey or jam. It also makes the BEST French toast . . . Bake it once and you will be hooked!

330g plain flour, plus extra for dusting and rolling
2 tbsp caster sugar
2 tsp rapid-rise yeast
½ tsp salt
80ml fresh orange juice
40g orange blossom honey
40ml pure sunflower oil
2 eggs
zest of an orange
½ tsp ground cardamom

FOR THE TOPPING
1 small egg, lightly beaten
1 tbsp sugar pearls or flaked almonds (optional)

- Prepare the dough by adding the flour, sugar, yeast and salt to the bowl of your stand mixer or a large mixing bowl. Stir to combine.

- Add the remaining ingredients and use a dough hook to mix them on a low speed until a shaggy dough forms.

- Continue mixing until the dough is smooth and forms a ball around the dough hook.

- Transfer the dough into an oiled bowl, cover with a clean tea towel and place somewhere warm to rise for 90–120 minutes, or until doubled in size.

- Weigh the dough and divide into four even pieces. Roll each piece into a ball. Flatten and roll each of these out with a rolling pin to form four small rectangles.

- Roll each rectangle into a log shape, pinching down the edges as you do. Use the palms of your hands to roll each piece out into a long rope. If the dough shrinks as you try to roll it, let it rest for a few minutes, so the gluten is allowed to relax.

- Repeat until you have four 30cm ropes.

- Place two of the strands vertically in front of you. Place the other two over the top horizontally to form a plus sign.

- Interlace them in a cross shape like a pie lattice. You will now have four pairs around the centre.

- Cross the strands of each of the four pairs, bottom over the top strand. This creates four new pairs.

Recipe Continues Overleaf
• • •

- Repeat the crossing of the strands until you reach the end of the ropes. Tuck the ends under to form a round loaf.

- Place the loaf on a greased air fryer liner and transfer to the basket. Brush with the beaten egg and leave to rise for 45–60 minutes.

- Brush the challah with egg wash once more just before baking and sprinkle with pearl sugar.

- Bake for 30 minutes at 170°C, checking whether the bread is browning too much halfway through. If it is, tent it with foil, weighing down the foil with a rack.

- Flip the bread over so it is bottom side up in the basket and remove the liner. Bake for a further 5–10 minutes, or until the bread is golden brown and sounds hollow when tapped on the underside. The internal temperature should be at least 90–93°C. Cool before slicing.

NOTES

* You can use stale challah bread to make the Churro French Toast Sticks on page 21.
* Store the cooled bread in a paper bag inside an airtight container or bread bin for 2–4 days. Alternatively you can freeze the sliced loaf and toast a slice from frozen whenever you get a craving!

Jam Doughnuts

PREP 20 mins
PROVE 2+ hrs
AIR FRY 10 mins
MAKES 8

Pillowy, sugary and jam-filled doughnuts that taste just like the real deal, minus the deep-frying. These are truly delicious and well worth the effort. You can use your favourite seedless jam or fruit curd to fill them.

FOR THE STARTER
120ml whole milk
20g bread flour (2 level tbsp)

FOR THE DOUGH
120ml whole milk
1 egg
55g unsalted butter,
    softened
1 tsp vanilla bean paste
350g bread flour
50g caster sugar
2 tsp rapid-rise yeast
½ tsp salt

FOR THE SUGAR-COATING
100g granulated sugar
60g unsalted butter, melted

FOR THE FILLING
10 tbsp seedless raspberry
    or strawberry jam

Make the starter

- Place the milk and flour in a saucepan and stir over a medium heat with a small balloon whisk until the whisk leaves a trail on the surface and you have a thick paste. Cover with cling film unless using straight away to prevent a skin forming on the surface.

Make the dough

- Add the milk to the saucepan containing the starter and heat until small bubbles appear around the edge. Allow this to cool until it is just tepid and stir in the egg, butter and vanilla. The butter should start melting in the residual heat.

- Measure the flour, sugar, yeast and salt into the bowl of a stand mixer fitted with a dough hook. Stir to combine.

- Pour in the contents of the saucepan while mixing on low speed. You should have a shaggy, sticky dough.

- Increase the speed slightly and mix for 2–4 minutes, or until the dough becomes elastic and starts forming a ball around the dough hook.

- Stretch a small piece of dough between your fingers – if it forms a see-through membrane without tearing it is ready to use.

First rise

- Mist the bowl with oil. Cover loosely with greased cling film and leave to rise for 60–90 minutes (depending on room temperature) or until doubled.

NOTE Make sure the liners are weighed down with the doughnuts or a small weight, otherwise the air will cause them to curl over or burn if they come into close contact with the heating element.

Recipe Continues Overleaf

Cut out the doughnuts/second rise

- Deflate the dough and tip on to a lightly floured worktop. Leave to rest for a few minutes, then roll out to 2½cm thick.

- Cut out rounds using a 7½cm round cutter, gathering dough scraps and rerolling as needed.

- Place on greased baking paper and cover loosely with greased cling film for 45–60 minutes, or until the doughnuts have doubled in size.

Air fry

- Preheat the air fryer to 180°C for 3 minutes. Place a wire rack in the air fryer basket, add a liner and spray with oil.

- Spray the doughnuts liberally with sunflower oil and place on the wire rack. Air fry in batches for 9–10 minutes, flipping halfway through.

Cover with sugar & fill

- Place the sugar in a shallow bowl. Brush the doughnuts with a little melted butter and dip in the sugar to coat. Allow to cool slightly.

- Fit a piping nozzle on a bag and fill with the jam. Poke a hole in the side of the doughnut and pipe in the jam. Serve immediately!

Beginner's Overnight Sourdough

PREP 15 mins
PROVE 8+ hrs
BAKE 30 mins
MAKES 2 small loaves

Sourdough bread can be a little intimidating but this stripped-down beginner's recipe cuts through most of the jargon. I promise you it is easy and the pride you will feel once you hold your warm sourdough baby in your hands is unparalleled.

FOR THE STARTER

60g mature starter at room temperature

60g flour

60g tepid water (filtered, or boiled and cooled tap water)

FOR THE SOURDOUGH

150g active starter (most of the starter you prepared earlier)

300g water (filtered, bottled or boiled and cooled tap water)

500g white bread flour

1 tbsp sugar

12g sea salt

2 tbsp fine semolina for the tin, or as needed

Feed the starter

- Feed a mature starter, then leave for 4–6 hours, or until doubled in size, bubbly and floating in water (the float test). Use the sourdough starter at its peak before it starts to sink again (you will see 'snail' trail on the sides of the jar when it starts to deflate).

Prepare the dough

- Combine the starter, water, flour, sugar and salt in a large mixing bowl. Use a dough whisk to stir until no dry streaks of flour remain. Cover with greased cling film and rest for 30 minutes.

- Stir the dough again; it should now be fully hydrated.

- Wet your hands (or use a dough whisk or spatula) and do a series of stretch and folds. Grab the underside of the dough and fold over the top.

- Rotate the bowl a quarter turn at a time and repeat until you have completed four sets of stretching and folding.

Bulk fermentation

- Overnight – transfer the dough into an oiled rectangular glass container, cover and leave to rise at room temperature overnight (8–10 hours) or in the fridge (10–12 hours) if it is a warm night. The timing is variable as the room temperature, humidity, strength of the starter and other factors play into it.

Divide, shape & rise

- Mist two 15cm tins or air fryer cake barrels with cake releases and sprinkle with semolina, shaking out any excess.

- Use wet hands or a scraper to divide the dough in half. Mist your worktop with water.

- Gently stretch one portion into a rough rectangle. Fold the dough into three sections, like a letter (letter fold).

- Rotate the dough and roll into a ball. Flip over, seam side down, and shape using your hands and a bench scraper into a small round loaf.

- Keep turning on the worktop, shaping between your hands and slightly tucking under until the loaf is smooth. Repeat with the second piece of dough.

Second rise

- Transfer into the prepared cake tins. Cover with greased cling film and rise until the dough springs back slowly, leaving a small dent when prodded gently with your finger. If it springs back quickly, you need to allow it to rise for a little longer.

Bake the sourdough

- Preheat the air fryer to 200°C for 5 minutes. Add a couple of ice cubes to the fryer to create steam.

- Bake for 10 minutes, reduce the temperature to 190°C and bake for a further 10 minutes. Use oven mitts to flip the loaf directly into the basket and bake for a further 8-10 minutes (28-30 minutes in total), or until the underside of the bread sounds hollow when tapped and the internal temperature is over 95°C. Cool the bread on a wire rack.

- Bake the second loaf in the same way but adjust the cooking time slightly. Since the air fryer will be hot, your loaf might bake in about 26–28 minutes.

- Wait until the bread has cooled before slicing.

NOTE To check whether your starter is ready, drop a spoonful into a glass of tepid water. If the starter floats you are good to go!

Sourdough Starter

This easy-going sourdough starter doesn't require you to discard any of it. It can be ready to bake in as little as a week, although it will become stronger with time. With a little love, your starter will reward you with beautiful bread for years to come. Now you just need to pick a name and make it part of your family.

750ml jar
white bread flour
water (ideally boiled and
   cooled tap water)
rye flour
sugar, caster or granulated

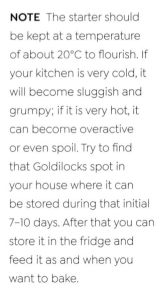

NOTE The starter should be kept at a temperature of about 20°C to flourish. If your kitchen is very cold, it will become sluggish and grumpy; if it is very hot, it can become overactive or even spoil. Try to find that Goldilocks spot in your house where it can be stored during that initial 7–10 days. After that you can store it in the fridge and feed it as and when you want to bake.

Day 1

- Put 25g white bread flour, 25g water, a generous pinch of rye flour and a tiny pinch of sugar into a clean jar. Stir well to combine until no dry streaks remain. Use a small flexible spatula to wipe the sides of the jar. Mark the level of the starter with a rubber band and loosely screw on the jar lid. Place in a warm spot in your kitchen, away from direct sunlight.

Days 2-4

- Repeat the feeding, ideally at the same time every day, adding flour, water and sugar, stirring well and adjusting the rubber band to the new level. You might see some bubbles forming during this time.

Days 5-7

- Continue the same feeding pattern. By now your starter should be bubbly and active, rising and falling in the jar.

Days 7+

- Once your starter is rising consistently to twice its volume after feeding, it is ready to bake with. Add a spoonful of the starter to a glass of tepid water. If the starter floats, then you are good to go!

- Once you start baking with your starter, you must always leave a small amount in the jar to feed and maintain. You can now store the starter in the fridge and take it out to feed the night before you want to bake with it again.

- Your starter will be OK in the fridge for up to two weeks before needing to be fed again. Read your recipe and feed the starter as instructed the night before. Sometimes you will need to wake up your starter with a couple of feedings before it comes back to full strength.

Buttermilk Cheese Scones

In North America these would be buttermilk biscuits . . . In the UK they are cheese scones. Either way, with their golden crunchy crust and perfectly soft crumb they taste delicious.

360g plain flour, plus extra
   for rolling
2 tbsp caster sugar
1 tbsp baking powder
½ tsp bicarbonate of soda
2 tsp sweet smoked paprika
1 tsp garlic granules
1 tsp salt
100g strong Cheddar
   cheese, grated
200ml buttermilk
40g mayonnaise

- Sift the flour, sugar, baking powder, bicarbonate of soda, paprika, garlic granules and salt into a mixing bowl.

- Stir in the grated cheese using two forks.

- Add the buttermilk and mayonnaise and stir until the dough is crumbly and forms clumps.

- Tip on to a lightly floured worktop and pat into a 3cm tall rectangle using floured hands.

- Cut out the scones with a floured 6cm fluted cutter, pressing straight down. Avoid twisting the cutter as that may cause your scones to rise unevenly.

- Gather any dough scraps and pat into shape to cut out additional scones.

- Cover the scones with a damp tea towel while you preheat the air fryer.

- Preheat the air fryer to 180°C. Place the scones on a liner in the basket, spaced apart to allow the air to circulate. Bake for 15–18 minutes or until the scones are well risen and golden.

Anadama Bread

PREP 20 mins
PROVE 3½ hrs
BAKE 35-40 mins
MAKES 1 small loaf

I first came across a recipe for Anadama bread in an American cookbook I bought at a second-hand shop. Once I baked it, I became enchanted with this sweet yet savoury dark bread. It has a cake-like crumb and tastes incredible toasted and spread with butter or paired with cheese.

125ml whole milk

35g fine cornmeal

25g unsalted butter

50g treacle

2 tbsp soft light brown sugar

60ml lager or stout

250g plain white flour, plus extra for dusting and rolling

1½ tsp rapid-rise yeast

1 tsp salt

2 tbsp fine cornmeal, for the cake barrel

- Combine the milk and cornmeal in a saucepan. Stir over a medium-low heat until the cornmeal thickens. Take off the heat, add in the butter and stir until it melts.

- Stir in the treacle, sugar and beer. Leave to cool until barely warm. Add the flour, yeast and salt to a mixing bowl or the bowl of your stand mixer fitted with a dough hook.

- Stir in the cooled cornmeal mixture, then beat for 5–7 minutes, until the dough becomes elastic. You can also knead it by hand for 10 minutes or so until it's pliable and no longer sticky.

- Grease the bowl with a little oil and turn the dough over so it is coated. Cover the bowl with greased cling film and leave the dough to rise for 2 hours. (This dough will not rise significantly.)

- Gently deflate the dough and form into a ball, dusting with flour if needed.

- Mist a 15cm air fryer cake barrel or cake tin with cake release. Add 2 tablespoons of cornmeal and shake so it coats the tin. Discard any excess. Place the loaf in the prepared tin and transfer to the basket of your air fryer. Leave it to rise for 90 minutes.

- Score the top of the loaf with a sharp knife. Place a couple of ice cubes in the air fryer basket next to your cake barrel, as the steam will help the initial rise of the bread.

- Bake at 170°C for 15 minutes. Reduce the temperature to 160°C and bake for 10 minutes. Lift the cake barrel out of the air fryer and invert the bread into the basket, bottom side up.

- Bake for a further 5–10 minutes or until the bread sounds hollow when tapped on the underside. The internal temperature should be at least 98°C. Cool the bread before slicing and serving.

Guinness Soda Bread

This easy soda bread is as dark as the stout it was named after. It's absolutely delicious spread with salted butter and served alongside stew or soup.

WET INGREDIENTS

240ml buttermilk

255ml Guinness (can use non-alcoholic)

30g butter, melted (or margarine)

3 tbsp molasses or treacle

DRY INGREDIENTS

260g wholemeal or spelt flour

90g rolled oats, plus 1 tbsp to sprinkle

3 tbsp dark brown sugar

2 tsp bicarbonate of soda

1 tsp baking powder

½ tsp salt

- Mist a 900g loaf tin with cake release and line with baking paper, letting the edges of the paper overhang slightly. Secure with clips if needed.

- Add all the wet ingredients to a bowl or large measuring jug and stir to combine.

- Measure the dry ingredients into a mixing bowl and stir to combine.

- Pour the wet ingredients into the dry and stir gently to combine until the batter is smooth and no dry streaks remain. Don't overwork the batter.

- Transfer the batter to the prepared tin and sprinkle with the oats.

- Preheat the air fryer to 180°C and bake for 45 minutes or until a skewer inserted in the centre comes out clean.

- Leave to cool inside the air fryer basket for 30 minutes or so.

- Lift out of the tin using the paper and transfer to a wire rack to cool completely before serving.

NOTE Cover the bread with foil after 15 minutes if it is browning too much.

Thank You

You would not be holding this book without the help and support of so many wonderful people.

© Thea Courtney

Thank you to Kay, my amazing agent, who believed in me from the start and put this whole whirlwind book adventure into motion.

To Dan, Aggie and everyone at Michael Joseph who have been so wonderful to work with – I could not have dreamed of a better or more welcoming team. Thank you to the irrepressible Georgie for the wonderful book design and art direction. Thank you to Jennie for the copy-editing and Jill for proofreading.

A huge thank you to Katie, Jess and Maria – my dream team of food stylists who kept cool under pressure and brought the recipes to life so beautifully.

Big thanks to Ant for the amazing photography and boundless enthusiasm during long shoot days. I am so glad we got to work together! Thank you to Sam for so wonderfully assisting. Thank you to Hannah for the prop styling.

A massive thank you to my husband Keith who has always been my greatest cheerleader. If it weren't for your support, this blogging lark would have never taken off. Thank you to my children, and toughest critics, Anya and Sam. I love you beyond measure.

My love of cooking and photography was instilled in me by my parents, and I could not be more grateful. I wouldn't be doing any of this if it weren't for you.

Finally, a heartfelt thank you to all of you, whether you have followed me through my blogging journey on Supergolden Bakes from the very beginning or joined now by picking up this book. I hope you enjoy these recipes as much as I loved creating them.

Index